When Money Destroys Nations

How Hyperinflation Ruined Zimbabwe,
How Ordinary People Survived, and
Warnings for Nations that Print Money

Philip Haslam
with Russell Lamberti

Front cover design by Ansh Deb Designs

Layout performed by Eugene Rijn Saratorio

WhenMoneyDestroys.com

Praise for *When Money Destroys Nations*

*"The simplicity, clarity, and great use of metaphors in this book
make* When Money Destroys Nations *a warning for the rest of the
world. It makes **me** ask: 'Will the U.S. be next?'"*

> — **Robert Kiyosaki**, Educator, Entrepreneur,
> Investor and Author of Rich Dad Poor Dad

*To understand the future you must first understand the past.
Haslam and Lamberti have done a great job at documenting
the Zimbabwean hyperinflation in an easily readable manner. Even
if you haven't studied economics or central banking, you'll be able
to understand what happens when countries print money and why
hyperinflation is coming to countries across the world, including the
US dollar.*

> — **Jeff Berwick**,
> founder and CEO of The Dollar Vigilante

*Haslam and Lamberti have produced a fascinating, accessible
account of how Zimbabweans actually lived (and died) during the
world's second-highest hyperinflation, one that dwarfed the German
hyperinflation of 1922–23. Yes, the peak daily inflation rate in
Zimbabwe in November 2008 was 98% – an economic tragedy
that Haslam and Lamberti skilfully bring to life.*

> — **Steve H Hanke**, professor of applied economics at the
> Johns Hopkins University in Baltimore and director
> of the Cato Institute's Troubled Currencies Project in
> Washington DC

An old and reliable adage states that one can learn either from experience or by reading what others have learned from experience. Most people have not lived through a monetary upheaval and have not experienced the disruptions to society when a currency goes bust. So to learn from others, When Money Destroys Nations *should be on everyone's reading list.*

> — **James Turk**, founder of GoldMoney and
> co-author of *The Money Bubble: What To Do Before
> It Pops*

We are rarely, if ever, exposed to what it is like to live through a hyperinflation. This is because it is so economically, socially and psychologically damaging. History records numerous runaway inflations, including ones in Germany, France, Russia, China and in Revolutionary America. With the spectre of hyperinflation looming in the future, When Money Destroys Nations *is a timely, accessible, and informative contribution to prepare people for the consequences.*

> — **Mark Thornton**, Senior Fellow of the Ludwig von
> Mises Institute and a Research and Fellow with the
> Independent Institute

I always appreciate literature that brings economic concepts to non-economists in a simple way that is fascinating to read. It is a measure of their knowledge on both the subject of Zimbabwe and hyperinflation that Haslam and Lamberti have been able to achieve the balance between using anecdotal evidence through countless interviews and a deep understanding of complex economic issues to achieve exactly that. This is a must-read for anyone who cares about holding their civil servants to account, the consequences of bad policies and how to prepare for the fallout.

— **George Glynos, MD** and
Chief Economist, ETM Analytics

In When Money Destroys Nations, Haslam and Lamberti have given a vivid account of how the Zimbabwean government's profligate spending, financed by central bank money printing, destroyed the living standards of people who either survived or fled the country's hyperinflation. Don't repeat the mistake of the millions of Zimbabweans who weren't prepared for what lay ahead. Pick up a copy of When Money Destroys Nations and learn about the factors that led to Zimbabwe's economic collapse, and use the framework that Haslam and Lamberti provide to help you monitor and understand hyperinflations. Consider implementing some of the authors' practical suggestions on how you can protect your family from the effects of a hyperinflationary economic collapse.

— **Chris Becker**, Economist and
Founder of the Mises Institute South Africa

When Money Destroys Nations

Philip Haslam

with Russell Lamberti

*To the millions of Zimbabweans who survived hyperinflation.
May this book do justice to the hardships you had to endure.*

Contents

Contents

Foreword
by Leon Louw

This is a splendid book with much to offer lay readers as economists. It is a rare example of scholarly substance combined with accessible narrative and human interest.

It explains much more than hyperinflation. Readers experience a rollercoaster ride through the ghastly horrors inflicted on entire populations by central bankers and politicians who use money to become diabolical oppressors. It provides disturbing insights into ominous parallels between Zimbabwe's hyperinflation and profligate polices that have become increasingly trendy in supposedly responsible countries, including the USA.

My colleague and friend, economist Vivian Atud, read the manuscript and was especially taken by the observation that 'governments have power to manipulate monetary policy but no power to manipulate the outcomes of their policies.'

The book has touching stories of how communities rallied to support destitute compatriots, how expatriates sent money and essential supplies to friends and relatives, and how trade was forced back to primitive barter. Tampons and toiletries, like much else, were scarce and used as currency substitutes.

Zimbabwe's hyperinflation was much more devastating than its liberation war or the oppression from which it liberated them. The book warns, often with Socratic and rhetorical questions, that money mischief is not easily understood, even by supposed experts. Ingenious disinformation and obfuscation deceives people into thinking perpetrators are rescuers. The US government's profligate response to their government-induced subprime

13

banking crisis, and the responses of Southern European governments to their 'sovereign debt' crisis are prime examples.

If this book is read by all who should read it, it will promote a substantially better-informed climate of opinion. Readers will be enriched by an appreciation of inflation as a form of taxation at best and plunder at worst. Hyperinflation is hyper-plunder of virtually all wealth. If more people understand a few basics, the propensity of central banks and governments to confiscate wealth by eroding currency values will be constrained. The book explains why the difference between inflation and hyperinflation is a matter of degree not principle; that the lesser of evils is still evil.

The penultimate section presents a compelling, if contentious, thesis to the effect that the Zimbabwe tragedy might be a portent of things to come elsewhere. It has a critique of US dollar dominance and of dangers emanating from exuberant confidence in the established view regarding inflation policy.

No lesser paper than the liberal Washington Post laments similarities between past hyperinflations and US monetary policy. It anguished about what 'great hyperinflation episodes…tell us about the Fed'. In the opposing ideological corner, the leading conservative-libertarian publication, Forbes, suggests that US hyperinflation might be 'imminent'.

Having alerted readers to the economic crises that might lie ahead, the book ends on a positive note with ideas on what individuals and governments can do to avoid or ameliorate hyperinflation. Much can be learned by readers 'in all walks of life', from ordinary folk to people who influence the course of events. It is clear from the book that every potential reader is one of the former and can be one of the latter.

Leon Louw
Executive director of the Free Market Foundation

Timeline of Zimbabwe's Hyperinflation

1965 Unilateral Declaration of Independence

1979 End of civil war

1980 First fully democratic elections

1980 -88 Zimbabwe finds favour with international lenders. Past economic success and newfound global acceptance masks underlying economic mismanagement, corruption and ethnic tension.

1989-96 Economic mismanagement intensifies. Bank lending rockets higher, saddling public and private sectors with large debts. Robert Mugabe entrenches personal power.

1997 Government makes major pension commitments to war veterans.
World Bank suspends its $100m loan facility to Zimbabwe.
Nov 14: Black Friday currency crash. Govt raises taxes, to cover large deficit. Large scale money printing begins.
Annual inflation rate: 20%

1998 Sep: Mugabe sends 11 000 troops into the DRC. Widespread protests in resistance to increased taxes. Government response is brutal but it decides to suspend the additional taxation programs. Numerous bank failures begin to hit the struggling economy. Annual inflation rate: 48%

1999 All external forms of funding are depleted, prompting full-scale money printing to take off in ernest. Official exchange rate for US dollars is fixed – black market for foreign currencies takes off. Annual inflation rate: 57%

2000 Failed referendum to change the constitution. Beginning of government land raids. Major foreign exchange shortages spark first Draconian foreign exchange controls on exporters. Annual inflation rate: 55%

2001 Banks begin to receive daily direct cash loans from the Reserve Bank of Zimbabwe. Widespread food riots errupt in response to soaring food prices. First major divergence between black market and official exchange rate creates major market distortions. Annual inflation rate: 112%.

2002 Price Control blitz - closure of many stores. Shortages of goods, electricity and water. The government's land reform progamme is accelerated after failed legal challenges. Annual inflation rate: 199%

2003 June: First major money

2004

Mar: The Reserve Bank of Zimbabwe raises interest rates dramatically to over 5000% in a desperate attempt to reduce rampant inflation. The move reduces inflation sharply, but precipitates a crash in the stock market and real estate.

Apr: Official exchange rate set equal to the black market rate for the last time. Annual inflation rate: 133%

shortages. Queues at bank ATMs and periodic runs on banks, creating a 30% premium paid on physical money vs bank deposits. Huge exodus of people from the country.

Dec: Gideon Gono appointed Governor of the Reserve Bank of Zimbabwe.

Annual inflation rate: 599%

2005 Interest rates lowered to "stimulate" the economy. Money printing continues. Official inflation likely heavily understated.

May: Government raids and plunders informal sector traders to enforce transaction control.

Annual inflation rate: 586%

2006

May: Annual inflation officially exceeds 1000%. All formal stores close - chronic food shortages.

August: Reserve Bank drops 3 zeros from the currency in the first of three re-denominations. Fuel coupons emerge as an alternative form of money. Annual inflation rate: 1,281%

2007 Zimbabwe enters dizzying rates of inflation. Feb: Reserve Bank of Zimbabwe declares inflation "illegal." Government printing press operating around the clock (printing 3 million notes per day by Nov). Draconian price controls forces most of the population into the informal sector.
Annual inflation rate: 66,212%

Acute hyperinflation **2008** pushes the country into economic shutdown.

Mar: Mugabe sworn in to his sixth term of office after presidential elections marred by high levels of political violence and vote rigging.

Jul: Reserve Bank drops 10 zeros off the currency.
Nov: Certain companies permitted to trade in alternative currencies - beginning of dollarisation.
Annualised inflation rate: 89.7 sextillion percent.

2009 Feb:Reserve Bank decision to drop 12 zeros from the currency is futile as the currency ceases to be used. Final collapse of the currency and full dollarisation. Shops fill up rapidly as formal trade resumes despite acute foreign currency shortages.

PART I

Money Printing: The Big Picture

Money from Heaven will be the path to Hell.

— Robert Wiedemer, economist

Daniel's warm eyes and greying hair contrasted with his tall, imposing frame. I could tell instantly that this senior banker was a successful, street-smart man. He was sitting across the table from me, explaining how clever it was for governments of the world to print money to repay their debts, and as the conversation turned to my plans for this book, a puzzled look came across his face.

'A book on Zimbabwe's hyperinflation,' he mused. 'Why on earth would you write about that?'

His question surprised me. Zimbabwe, a once-prosperous nation, had been utterly ruined in a few short years – not by war or natural disaster, but by unrestrained money printing; the very action Daniel was advocating.

I recounted to him what had happened in Zimbabwe that led it towards its extraordinary economic meltdown. As the government printed money to pay its debts, prices began to soar until stores everywhere emptied and everyone became hungry. Water supplies ran dry and electricity cut out. No one could get any fuel. The Zimbabwean way of life was destroyed; ordinary people became destitute and millions fled the country.

The account fascinated Daniel. As we shook hands and prepared to leave, he paused and asked, 'With the vast money printing programmes in developed countries today, could any of them ever become like Zimbabwe?'

*   *   *

It's a sobering question. The wealthiest countries of the world are printing money on an unprecedented scale – the very same strategy that led Zimbabwe to a predictable and severe economic disaster. This book examines the causes of Zimbabwe's economic collapse, how it impacted people practically, and what lessons it holds for nations around the world.

In researching Zimbabwe's tragic story, I interviewed people from every sector of society. I met with senior central bank officials. Business leaders imparted their strategies. Farmers spoke about their heartache and pensioners told me their desperate stories. I received input from people from all walks of life. Over 75 Zimbabweans shared their detailed experiences with me. Their personal stories of hardship, resilience and ingenuity are heartbreaking and inspiring. Most have put themselves at risk by talking to me, so I've changed their identities in the many quotes throughout the book.

I then partnered with another economist, Russell Lamberti, who has provided critical and substantial input.

- In Part I, we unveil what happened in Zimbabwe, explaining why and how debt and money printing cause economic crises.
- In Part II, we show how hyperinflation practically affected people from all walks of life, telling the dramatic yet heartfelt stories of ordinary Zimbabweans.
- Finally, in Part III, we discuss how money printing threatens to destroy the major currencies of the world and how this could affect you.

In total, from 1980 to 2009 Zimbabwe issued 82 different denominations of currency notes. Throughout the book, we have included each note in the order that they were issued, as visual aids to the inflation story.

Zimbabwe's story gives us critical clues from which we have built a powerful framework for broader application to other countries generally. Much of the material has been developed from the numerous interviews I conducted. While the principles established in this book are based predominantly on this particular case study, we also draw on other such cases in history as well as from sound economic principles. While no two episodes in economic history are ever identical, we have found very similar patterns emerging during different historical cases of hyperinflation and these provide guidelines to assessing the threat of hyperinflation in other countries.

This is a rich and wide-ranging theme and we recommend that you read further on this topic. You can find a list of recommended reading and useful resources, as well as advisory services at WhenMoneyDestroys.com.

We trust that, after this journey, you'll never think the same way about money and your future again.

Chapter 1

Bernanke's Panic

What has been will be again, what has been done will be done again; there is nothing new under the sun.

— Ecclesiastes 1:9

September 2008. Autumn. New York. It was a race against time. Panic had spread across world markets in one of the scariest weeks in financial history. The United States – and therefore the entire world – was on the verge of an economic collapse that only two men could stop.

For the previous 18 months, American house prices had fallen, putting a huge strain on banks. A few major multinational banks had collapsed. First was Northern Rock in England, then Bear Stearns in New York, followed by a host of others. The financial system began to bend under the strain as 52 banks across the globe either declared bankruptcy, were nationalised or merged with other banks in emergency takeovers. Trust in the financial system was evaporating.

Earlier in September 2008, Freddie Mac and Fannie Mae, two massive American mortgage lenders, were brought to the brink of insolvency. The authorities acted quickly and fully nationalised them in the hope that this would stop the financial rot from spreading. It didn't.

Sunday, 14 September 2008. By this point, the fourth and fifth largest investment banks in the United States, Merrill Lynch and Lehman Brothers, were in crisis. In an attempt to stop further insolvencies, the regulators had been negotiating over the weekend for other banks to take them over. They managed to force Bank of America to acquire Merrill Lynch, announcing it in the morning papers. But they couldn't find a buyer for Lehman Brothers, despite desperate attempts to do so.

US Treasury Secretary Henry Paulson and Federal Reserve Chairman Ben Bernanke had been working around the clock to avert disaster – a disaster, many would later argue, made possible by the very economic policies that Bernanke and Paulson had implemented in preceding years. The pressure was relentless. Paulson was having sleepless nights and the stress led to a nasty gastric condition that caused him to throw up multiple times a day. He knew the dire consequences and later said of the failed Lehman Brothers sale, 'I wasn't quite sure what to say. I was gripped with fear. I called [my wife] and said, "Wendy, you know, I feel that the burden of the world is on me and that I failed and it's going to be very bad, and I don't know what to do, and I don't know what to say. Please pray for me."'[1]

Monday, 15 September 2008. At 1:45 a.m., Lehman Brothers filed for bankruptcy. The news was a dagger to the heart of financial markets. Banks around the world were bleeding money as depositors withdrew everything they could. The American banking and financial system was collapsing and would potentially drag down the entire global financial system, with dramatic consequences.

Tuesday, 16 September 2008. Market mayhem ensued. American International Group (AIG), an enormous multinational insurer, was in dire

straits. It insured banks for certain kinds of losses, and after the collapse of Lehman Brothers, the company didn't have the money to pay out on its insurance – it was broke. During the helter-skelter of financial panic, many believed that AIG's bankruptcy would push the markets over the edge. It was unthinkable. Unwilling to take a chance, Ben Bernanke approved an injection of US$85 billion of newly printed money into AIG from the Federal Reserve.

Wednesday, 17 September 2008. Financial markets continued to unravel. The other investment banks were cracking under the pressure. Stock market prices plunged. Many expected another massive investment bank, Morgan Stanley, to be the next in line in a host of bank failures.

Thursday, 18 September 2008. The break-the-glass rescue plan that Paulson and Bernanke devised had been in discussion for nine months. Time was of the essence, and at 4:30 p.m. New York time, the pair hastily convened a meeting of congressional leaders. The US government would borrow US$700 billion from local and foreign lenders to give it in various ways as bailouts to troubled banks.

The lengthy meeting was attended by President George Bush and then presidential hopefuls Barack Obama and John McCain. As deadlock set in, Ben Bernanke warned, 'If we don't act immediately, we will not have an economy by Monday.' George Bush warned that 'if money isn't loosened up, this sucker could go down'. Henry Paulson even got down on one knee, begging the leaders to approve the plan.[2] As the committee talked through the night, the urgency of the situation became clear. They eventually put aside their various political differences and agreed to the plan, which they called the Troubled Asset Relief Program or TARP for short.

Friday, 19 September 2008. The paperwork for the TARP bailout plan was hurriedly put together to be passed into law, and with a calm and assured façade it was announced on CNBC at 3:01 p.m. New York time.

The plan dressed the immediate wounds of the financial system, but it was only a hurried patch job. Stock markets continued to go haywire as banks worldwide continued taking strain, and it was clear that the authorities needed to come up with more money. Within a few weeks, on 26 November 2008, the US Federal Reserve initiated a plan that would eventually see it print a staggering US$1.7 trillion (US$1 700 000 000 000) of new money within 18 months, effectively giving it to the banks as a bailout. The money printing plan became known as quantitative easing, or simply QE (we discuss the detail of how quantitative easing works in the endnotes[3]).

In the weeks and months to come, central banks around the world, from Britain to China to Dubai to Japan, followed suit with their own money printing and bank bailout schemes. By 2014, America had printed over US$3.5 trillion since the 2008 crisis, not only to bail out the banks but also to fund its increasingly indebted government. To illustrate how large this number is, with the US$3.5 trillion, in 2008, the Federal Reserve could have theoretically been able to purchase all the listed companies in the UK, Germany and India combined![4]

Is Money Printing Really That New?

By the time of the crisis, the major economies of the world had incurred so much debt that those in charge of economic policy were pressed into a corner to print money on a large scale to 'save the system'. In the relief of avoiding a worldwide economic meltdown, few stopped to ask the question, 'What is the long-term impact of all this money printing?' Did the Federal Reserve really save the global financial system, or did it merely postpone the crisis, making the problems bigger in the process?

As the fires of the financial crisis burned in New York, these questions were being answered 12 500 kilometres away, on the other side of the world, in a small country in Africa. Zimbabwe's currency, the Zimbabwe dollar, was experiencing its final death pangs. By mid-November 2008, the same month the US started printing vast sums of money, annual inflation in Zimbabwe soared to an unfathomable 89 700 000 000 000 000 000 000%. That's 89.7 sextillion per cent! The country had reached the culmination of its money printing excesses: *hyperinflation and total economic collapse.*

The collapse had been two decades in the making. Eleven years earlier, after nearly a decade of economic mismanagement, Zimbabwe experienced its own major financial crisis. In response, the desperate Zimbabwean government chose to print money to save its economy. With congratulatory slaps on the back, the government was sure it had liberated the country from its debts. But as it continued to print money, Zimbabwe descended into a deep, dark chaos. Dizzying rates of inflation totally destroyed the once-prosperous economy.

Why Study Hyperinflation?

The more things change, the more they stay the same.

– French proverb

Zimbabwe's sad story gives us clues to the consequences of money printing and how it impacts the lives of ordinary families and communities. Some of the Zimbabweans I interviewed had this to say:

The currency died a slow and painful death. We were all expecting the economy to collapse in an instant – the warning signs were evident but the 'Big Moment' only came years later. Like the half-life deterioration of radioactive waste, our situation became progressively worse. Each year the situation got more dire. And every year we'd reflect, 'This was the worst of all possible years – surely the economy is going to improve.' But it never did. It just got worse.

– Farmer based in Harare, Zimbabwe

In the beginning, it started out simply with prices rising. But then came the money shortages. Then food shortages. We lost everything we had and by the end we were working multiple jobs but living in abject poverty. Slowly but progressively our lifestyle evaporated away.

– Mother of two

My parents retired shortly before the collapse. They were well off financially, having saved their whole lives, and their retirement plans stood them in great stead. Within a matter of years, they had lost everything. They didn't even have enough to put food on the table.

— Zimbabwean living in South Africa

Had these people known the challenges they would face from the time the central bank started printing money on a large scale, they could have prepared – and they *should* have prepared.

What Is Hyperinflation and What Causes It?

Hyperinflation is when prices surge uncontrollably with little respite, destroying an economy in the process. Hyperinflation is caused by the unrestrained creation of money to fund a government's expenses – either by printing new paper money or creating digital money (both of which we refer to as 'money printing'). Sooner or later, this leads to a collapse in confidence in the nation's currency. It is a tremendously personal event and affects all people in an economy, relegating most to poverty. In Zimbabwe, even people who understood very little about national finances came to know what hyperinflation was.

Hyperinflation can happen anywhere. It has occurred all over the world – in Germany, Greece and China, as well as in countries in Eastern Europe,

Africa and South America. Paper money printing technology (and later digital money creation) has made the twentieth century the greatest inflation period in history. While there have been significant inflation periods throughout history, the most comprehensive study of hyperinflation to date, conducted in 2012 by professor Steve Hanke and Nicholas Krus, reveals as many as 52 incidences of hyperinflation since 1920.[5] That is an average of more than one incident of hyperinflation every two years. Inflation is not a new phenomenon. Ancient Rome, seventeenth century France, and eighteenth century America all experienced terrible inflation episodes. In each instance, hyperinflation varied in duration and ferocity, but always left an unmistakable footprint of devastation on the nation.

Even with these global experiences of hyperinflation, money printing is currently 'all the rage' among central bankers. Never before have we seen such a readiness to print money. Japan and the United States are leading the charge in money printing, followed closely by Britain and Europe. Not to be outdone, China and Switzerland have been marching on with their own enormous money printing programmes.

As countries around the world print money hand over clenched fist, the signs are ominous. Zimbabwe's experience is a blueprint and a warning to governments and citizens alike. You can learn from its mistakes and respond. This book shows you how.

Chapter 2

Beautiful Zimbabwe

Why is it you can never hope to describe the emotion Africa creates? You are lifted. Out of whatever pit, unbound from whatever tie, released from whatever fear. You are lifted and you see it all from above.

    − Francesca Marciano

I first experienced Zimbabwe in 1987 at the young age of eight. It was late autumn when we left our home city of Johannesburg for our family getaway. As we flew into Zimbabwe, orange and red trees flooded the horizon under hazy blue skies.

The plane touched down and as the doors opened, a fog of dense, subtropical heat greeted my youthful excitement. The world's largest waterfall, the mighty Victoria Falls, beckoned. The holiday was a blur of adventure characterised by sunset cruises up the Zambezi River, soaked viewings of the awe-inspiring falls and Z$1 sodas drunk out of dew-drenched glass bottles. At that early age, I was struck by the untamed beauty of the land and the disarming gentleness of the people.

Fast-forward 14 years to 2001. I returned to Zimbabwe, this time to celebrate my friend's wedding. We were having his bachelor party on the shores of Lake Kariba in northern Zimbabwe, in a luxurious holiday house 20 metres from the water – as close to the wild as you could get. At night, five or six wild hippos would wander up from the lake to graze on the outside lawn. This place had ways to send a man off from bachelorhood that Las Vegas could only dream of. During one festive evening, our friend was sent to stalk the hippos, with the strict instruction to get as close as possible without being attacked. Our half-naked bachelor crept to within 2 metres of an unsuspecting hippo before both of them fled in terror!

Amidst our revelries, we capitalised on what were, for us, fantastically cheap prices. At the time, the exchange rate reflected the early stages of currency collapse. We were poor students but still managed to afford a large lakeside house, each with our own room and hot tub Jacuzzi en suite.

With housekeeping, meals and drinks, the trip (excluding airfares) cost us each US$2 a day. An ice-cold soda now cost us Z$20 at the lake store, a full 20 times what my family and I had paid in 1987.

While the undertones of inflation discord and political discontent were distant rumbles to our travelling party, I couldn't help but sense the increasing poverty among the locals. The US$10 tip that we gave our housekeeper would see to her and her family's basic needs for the next few weeks.

Six years passed before my next visit in 2007 for another wedding, this time in the capital city Harare. A lot had changed. The blaze of hyperinflation was roaring out of control. The dusty, potholed streets and empty stores betrayed a nation in disintegration. Worthless money littered the streets. Gone was the bustle of business activity. The distinctive odour of want filled the air. A bottle of soda now cost Z$87 billion.

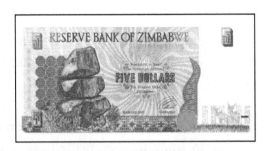

*   *   *

'You can meet him behind the bar,' he whispered.

I was enquiring at the post office as to where I could exchange foreign currency shortly after I had arrived on my second wedding trip.

The skinny clerk had to come around the desk to speak in hushed tones. 'The dealer only operates at night so you'll have to wait. But make sure no one is following you when you go.'

Later that evening, and three guarded doors later, I found the dealer sitting in a smoky room. His glazed eyes revealed years of trial. We exchanged pleasantries, and once he was sure I wasn't a policeman, he pulled out a beaten black metal case filled with packs of money.

We completed our secret trade by candlelight, and I marched, heart pounding, with long, rapid strides to our car. I had just had my first experience of Zimbabwe's black market. The idea of a night in a police cell inspired perspiration and constant checks over my shoulder – I wanted to get out of there.

In a few short years, the entire culture had shifted from one of economic hope to fear, suspicion and corruption. Zimbabwe was being ravaged by unrestrained money printing.

As I boarded my departing flight two days later, I felt a strong sense of relief to be going home. My bed that night was extra soft, and I slept in peace and the comfort of stable prices.

In early 2013, five years after the collapse of the Zimbabwe dollar, I returned to Zimbabwe, this time to study the personal effects of hyperinflation. I arrived on a mission to hear from the people themselves what had happened and how they had survived. In the many interviews I conducted, people shared heartbreaking stories of personal suffering. And yet showed tremendous creativity and innovation in coping with extreme economic stress. The scars of the nation carry stories few know about yet everyone should hear.

The lessons learned the hard way by ordinary people in Zimbabwe – parents, friends, teachers, employees and business leaders – are for one and all. They paint the grim picture of what happens when governments print money with the spectacular unreservedness that many are doing around the world today.

The Breadbasket of Africa

Prior to the hyperinflation, Zimbabwe was full of natural wealth and economic opportunity.

The country is landlocked, bordered by four countries in the heart of southern Africa. It is crowned with the natural beauty and wild heritage of all things African, including a population of peaceable, well-educated and hard-working people.

To the north lies the Zambezi River that pours over the Victoria Falls I had visited as a child. The river, which acts as the nation's northern border to Zambia, rages and ebbs on its way to the Indian Ocean, but not before it

decants into one of the largest man-made lakes in the world, Lake Kariba, venue of our bachelor celebrations.

Zimbabwe's fertile soil is watered by great summer thundershowers and many winding rivers. The fragrant red earth has long been the love of Zimbabwean people.

Below the surface, the ground is rich in minerals, including diamonds, gold, platinum, nickel, iron, silver and coal. The country is blessed with a plethora of wildlife, and the vast nature reserves capture something unique of the African wilderness.

This is a beautiful country.

How Did Zimbabwe Get to Where it is Today?

Zimbabwe has relatively few people groupings; it is almost entirely made up of the Shona people of the north and east, the Ndebele people of the west and south, and the English, who colonised it in the nineteenth century. Combined today, it is difficult to find a kinder group of people anywhere across the earth. Their richness in community became the backbone of survival during the hyperinflation years.

As the beauty of Zimbabwe shines out, the shadow of its darker history lies in stark contrast. Indeed, Zimbabwe is a land of contradiction. Its high peaks are contrasted with low valleys. Peaceful communities are juxtaposed with rogue leaders. Despair alongside hope, and faith alongside suffering. It carries lessons – born out of simple, but costly, errors – for the world.

Zimbabwe[6] was occupied by Britain from the late 1880s until the 1960s. With the independence movement sweeping across Africa during the 1960s, many countries revolted against colonial control, and Britain was keen to avoid a messy divorce with its Zimbabwean colony.

Independence negotiations began in the early 1960s and the British were adamant that to receive full independence from the crown, the country had to establish full democratic rights for all, including its black citizens. These talks broke down with the local white-controlled political movement under Ian Smith unhappy with giving black Zimbabweans the vote. Ultimately, the local white movement made a Unilateral Declaration of Independence (UDI) in 1965 and severed ties with the British.

The UDI caused international outrage, particularly in Britain, which pushed for global sanctions against Zimbabwe until such time as the whole population had the right to vote.

Zimbabwe developed rapidly despite the sanctions, trading with its much larger (but internationally ostracised) neighbour, South Africa. Its agricultural business sector exported produce to the rest of Africa, Britain and Europe. The country developed sophisticated infrastructure including large hydroelectric dams, municipal water systems, roads and hospitals. Local farms flourished as commercial farmers developed expertise in tobacco, cotton, timber and most of the major grains. Zimbabwe became known as the breadbasket of Africa as the level of production far outstripped the needs of its population. Booming agriculture helped develop complementary industries such as textiles, fertiliser and transport. Its banking sector developed during this time in line with Western banking

standards, becoming based on a reserve banking model with fractional reserve lending by commercial banks. Zimbabwe's level of development during this period was remarkable given the sanctions imposed upon it by the rest of the world.

The Unilateral Declaration of Independence came with a dark side. Not only had it denied access to vote for most of the population, but it increasingly oppressed political parties representing black people who were agitating for change. Eventually, the political conflict descended into a long and costly civil war.

After 15 years of brutal combat, the parties moved to form a truce. By 1980, a conference chartering the terms for peace convened in London. The parties agreed on terms that led to the first universal elections in the country. The new president, Robert Mugabe, responded with reconciliation and forgiveness towards his white predecessors. The elections were acclaimed as faultless, and Zimbabwe became the darling of the international community.

But while the world was singing Zimbabwe's praises, beneath the surface, the Mugabe administration began to make unwise economic decisions and, slowly but surely, centralised power around itself and its leader. Specialist military units were developed and became politicised. Cracks in national unity began to show.

This newfound power gave the state increased hunger for spending money, and the state's consumption habit grew, corroding Zimbabwe's dynamism. This was the start of a dangerous economic disease that ultimately devastated the Zimbabwe dollar and collapsed the economy.

Beautiful Zimbabwe in a Nugget

Prior to its economic collapse, Zimbabwe was loaded with potential. It had abundant infrastructure and trade was booming. Known as the breadbasket of Africa because of its massive agricultural industry, it brimmed with possibility and opportunity. And yet increasing control by the government, militarisation and unbridled state consumption created a political and economic infection that would lead to the ultimate death of the currency and the collapse of the economy.

Chapter 3

Storm Warnings

There has never occurred a hyperinflation in history which was not caused by a huge budget deficit of the state.

— **Professor Peter Bernholz**, hyperinflation economist

When national debts have once been accumulated to a certain degree, there is scarce, I believe, a single instance of their having been fairly and completely paid. The liberation of the public revenue, if it has ever been brought about at all, has always been brought about by a bankruptcy...frequently by a pretended payment.

— **Adam Smith**, The Wealth of Nations

The Build-up of a Storm

We crossed Zimbabwe's border at dawn. The first beams of sunlight had begun to warm the African horizon, illuminating the unfolding landscape. It was my second trip to Zimbabwe, and the three of us, plus mountains of wedding luggage, squeezed into an old Toyota Camry.

'I'm glad we have air con,' my brother sighed as the summer sun baked our meandering tar highway.

The drive was long but beautiful. Random wooded hills punctuated the green landscape, and white cotton clouds dotted the sky. As our day progressed, the rolling hills flowed by as a blur of grassland and wilderness. At each stop, loud crickets sang their shrill greetings. We were in Africa for sure.

The day progressed with the sky growing ominously darker. The clouds had grown from their small white wisps into an imposing weather system. A large storm was developing ahead.

The first giant raindrop bulleted on to our windscreen; then came the barrage. The assault was so fierce we had to pull over as the sky emptied its arsenal of rain and hail over our hapless Camry. The storm crashed and boomed its battle symphony. Violent. Terrifying. Majestic. And over within an hour.

Throughout the day, we had noticed the telltale signs of the coming storm. First, the billowing black clouds, brightened by the occasional flash on the horizon, then the deep rumblings of thunder, followed by gusty winds rustling the leaves. If you're attuned to it, an electric scent hangs in the air just before a storm. And if you don't find shelter quickly, you'll be caught in the torrent.

Just like the great storms of Africa, hyperinflation builds up with telltale signs, with a final deluge of paper notes and prices soaring out of control.

How Did Zimbabwe Go from 'Normal' to 'Hyperinflationary'?

What went wrong in this land of endless potential? Can we learn from the precursors to the Zimbabwe crisis? Are there principles that apply to other countries of similar great potential? What are the signs to look for, and can we see storm clouds on the horizon?

The answers to these questions are both simple and complex. Yes, we absolutely can learn from the precursors to the Zimbabwean crisis. Hyperinflation isn't something that just happens. You don't wake up one morning to find that your country slipped into it overnight. It gathers momentum and builds over time, with key warning signs.

In another sense, we must always remain humble in our predictive abilities. Hyperinflation is never a neat, high-precision event. It is a chaotic process. It is a fundamentally complex socio-economic phenomenon. Some hyperinflations are worse than others. Some political leaders make the right choices in the tough times and others do not. Some hyperinflations build quickly and others slowly. Yet, as complex as these events may be, it would be foolish to ignore the warnings. There are common precursors to hyperinflation – warnings of an impending storm.

Typically, government spending increases to a point where it is a significant component of an economy. It runs up large debts over a prolonged period and increasingly uses money printing as a source of funding. If debts keep mounting and are not paid off, a time comes when lenders lose confidence in the ability of the government to repay, and withdraw their financial support, resulting in financial panic and loss of value of the currency. At this stage, the government runs out of debt-funding alternatives, and the weaker currency causes the cost of imports to rise. The government then makes the political decision to use money printing as its primary form of financing after exploring all tax options available to it. This pushes the country down an inflation path that cascades into hyperinflation.[7]

Two leading Harvard professors of economics and advisors to the International Monetary Fund, Kenneth Rogoff and Carmen Reinhart, have done extensive analysis of government debt after financial crises.[8] They show that government debt typically spirals out of control after a major financial crisis. At some stage, these increased debts cause a government debt panic, leading to a subsequent currency crisis. Zimbabwe's episode certainly supports these findings. A financial crisis led the country down a debt spiral that culminated in the ultimate currency crisis: hyperinflation.

In analysing Zimbabwe, we've divided these precursors into three specific categories: (1) Running Up Debts, (2) Financial Panic, and (3) the Political Decision to Print Money.

1. Running Up Debts

Behind a glossy veneer, Robert Mugabe's government was making poor policy decisions from the early 1980s, decisions that would allow the storm clouds to build large and dark by the late 1990s. The government's spending and indebtedness rose steadily. It made pension promises that the country couldn't afford, got involved in a costly war, and developed an unhealthy addiction to offshore loans.

1.1. False promises: large pensions and social security

Robert Mugabe's government came to power on the back of a liberation struggle. After the civil war ended in December 1979, rehabilitation of the war veterans became a primary political concern. Few of these veterans had any skills that could be gainfully employed. The government established a social security scheme called the War Veteran Compensation Fund to provide disability payouts to war veterans. Over the years, the fund was depleted by corrupt government officials, and by 1996, the kitty had run dry.

With no further compensation, the war veteran movement began organised marches to petition for additional payouts, increasing in intensity and strength through the first six months of 1997. They were a nuisance pressure group to the ruling party and Mugabe responded by approving a new monthly pension plan for all war veterans that equated to around double the average monthly salary of a civil servant in Zimbabwe at the time.

With the cost of living rising, other groups began to ask, 'What about us?' Social security obligations were firmly on the political agenda, becoming a primary source of excessive state spending.

These obligations hadn't been planned for and they particularly alarmed the country's foreign lenders who were concerned with how these social security plans would be funded.

1.2. Military misadventures: costly war in the Democratic Republic of Congo

In addition to these pension expenses, in 1998 Robert Mugabe sent 11 000 troops into the Democratic Republic of Congo (DRC) on a peace-keeping mission to support the leader at the time, Laurent Kabila. The DRC was facing civil war as rebel forces had destabilised the country.

As Mr Mugabe was to find out, wars are costly excursions. The war expenses added another burden on the already floundering public finances and only increased the concerns of the international investment community, who feared that they would lose their money.

1.3. Debt sweat: pressure from lenders

After the country gained its independence, the international community welcomed Zimbabwe into its fold with open arms. Zimbabwe had an almost perfect credit record internationally because of its strong farming and mining sectors, and the IMF and the World Bank began to lend heavily to the country, arm-wrestling the government into making various structural economic reforms. These structural reforms served to bolster the already sophisticated banking system that had been developed in Zimbabwe.

Based on normal fractional reserve bank lending, the government and the banks started to increase the supply of money in the economy at a much more rapid rate. From 1990, the money supply (known in economic circles as M1) nearly tripled in four years, and by 1997 it had almost tripled again.

In 1997, the World Bank was in the process of arranging a US$100 million loan facility for Zimbabwe when it heard the news of the huge pension expense about to be incurred. Within a month of the pension being declared, the World Bank withdrew its facility pending further detail on how these pensions would be funded and how the proceeds from its loans would be spent. It had become concerned by the increased spending

and lax attitude towards debt and money printing. In response, Mugabe's government stopped making debt repayments to the World Bank – an effective default –and suspended the economic reform initiatives it had started.

2. Financial Panic

2.1. Market crash: Black Friday

The breakdown in the relationship with Zimbabwe's funders was the forerunner of a market collapse. Brewing investor distrust boiled to panic point, and on Friday, 14 November 1997, the Zimbabwe dollar plummeted, losing 75% of its value in one day. That day, known as Black Friday, was a definitive turning point. Years of complacent mismanagement found expression in one panic-stricken moment. The day triggered a continued fall in the value of the currency and the Zimbabwe dollar was never to recover.

Black Friday was economically catastrophic. One woman who owned an import business in Zimbabwe at the time said this:

> *I remember the crash like it was yesterday – it was a Friday morning in the middle of spring. I was sitting at my desk drinking my third cup of coffee when our purchasing manager rushed through to tell me the news. I was in meetings for the rest of the day and he came through five or six times to give updates on how far the currency value had fallen.*

We ran a small business in printing and we imported all our branding and technology to sell locally. Our input costs were based in US dollars and the crash practically destroyed our business. The exchange rate kept on getting worse and worse. From then on, everything changed. We eventually had to close up shop.

With the spectacular drop in the value of the Zimbabwe dollar, the cost of the country's imports soared overnight, which required much more foreign currency, already scarce with the international loans being withdrawn. The currency continued to plummet.

It wasn't the only market crash. The country would have many subsequent crashes as it spun down its debt and money printing vortex. In 2000, the economy experienced a major contraction from a land confiscation and redistribution project. In 2003, it had a major banking crisis. Crisis after crisis followed as money printing escalated.

2.2. Debt spiral: maxing out the national credit card

Black Friday exposed a harsh reality: the emperor had no clothes. Lenders could now see how exposed Zimbabwe really was, facing the threat of bankruptcy.

With the currency falling in value and import costs rising rapidly, the government had to find an extra 55% in its 1998 budget or be forced to cut spending dramatically. Mugabe responded by raising taxes but came against strong resistance as food riots erupted in the major towns.

The government's reaction to the riots was brutal – ten people were killed, and hundreds were assaulted and arrested.[9] Wanting to avoid further confrontation, the government removed the additional taxes. Increasing taxes was no longer a viable political option for funding public expenses.

By 1999, the government's financial mismanagement was now plainly evident. All foreign donor organisations had suspended aid to Zimbabwe. Assistance and funding in any form of foreign exchange had largely dried up. Soaring government debt and trade deficits only damaged confidence in Zimbabwe further, and the currency continued to weaken. Trying to keep pace with rising costs, the government exhausted every avenue to fund its expenditures as debt spiralled out of control. In particular, the cost of importing critical goods such as fuel into the economy became astronomically expensive.

Chart 1 shows how Zimbabwe's government debt burden rose considerably in the years preceding Black Friday and then accelerated higher after the crisis.

Given the extent of inflation, we have put the chart in a log-scale. At each point where the graph crosses a horizontal line, the total government debt increased tenfold.

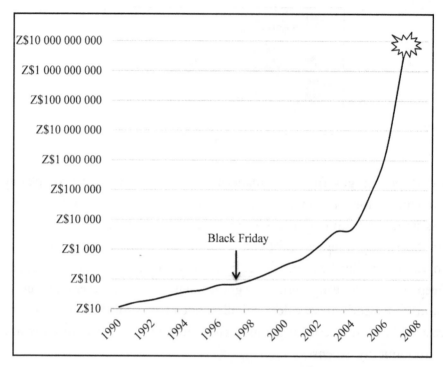

Chart 1: Zimbabwe general government debt
1990–2007, Z$ billions (Log Scale)
Source: International Monetary Fund, St. Louis Federal Reserve
Bank, Philip Haslam & Russell Lamberti

3. The Political Decision to Print Money

*In many senses, yes it was the Reserve Bank of Zimbabwe that caused
the hyperinflation. But it didn't have any option. It was driven by the
government's wishes. Monetary policy was driven by political policy.*

– Reserve Bank of Zimbabwe employee

3.1. Choosing to print money

Government finances were floundering. The options available to Mugabe's government had expired. The financial malaise was wrecking the economy, and tax revenues were dwindling. The desperate government could respond in one of two ways. Either it could reduce its expenses dramatically by closing down many government services and laying off state employees, or it could print the Zimbabwe dollars it needed.

Prior to 1997, the normal restraints for printing money embedded in the Reserve Bank's operating procedures had begun to erode. When the value of the currency crashed on Black Friday, the Reserve Bank, compelled by the government, completely discarded any residual money printing discipline.

This second option – to print money – had comparatively little immediate negative effect and was by far the most politically convenient. And yet, as the country would later experience, the eventual effects were far more destructive.

After 1997, and especially after 2000, the amount of money printing went into orbit, rising exponentially as the malaise of hyperinflation took ever greater hold.

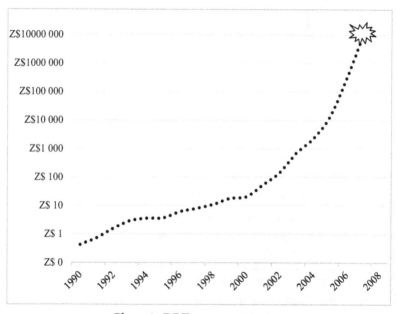

Chart 2: RBZ money printing
1990–2007, Z$ billions (Log Scale)
Source: International Monetary Fund, St. Louis Federal
Reserve Bank, Philip Haslam & Russell Lamberti

Chart 2 shows the extent of money printing in Zimbabwe. It is in log-scale: every time the graph crosses a horizontal line, the amount of money in the economy increased tenfold.

The political decision to print money wasn't only directed at funding the government. In addition, banks also needed newly printed notes to stay afloat. Banks had lent out a lot more, relative to the money they had on hand. They were very exposed to a bank run (when depositors lose confidence in the security of their deposits and all try to withdraw their money *en masse*). Since the banks held a fraction of the actual money relative to the amount of money that reflected on their books, the banks didn't have enough money to repay depositors. The central bank had to give these banks newly printed money to bail them out.

Initially, as banks received bailouts with newly printed money, they hoarded it to restore their financial health. This meant it could take quite some time for newly printed money to find its way into the broader economy, delaying its inflation effect.

Later on, however, as inflation began to increase, banks realised that the value of their money holdings was decreasing. They began to spend it on things that would hold value. The money that was originally printed and given to the banks now began to enter the economy, causing a much greater rise in inflation.

3.2. Increased government control

With the rising tide of new money coming into the economy and inflation beginning to escalate, people began to ask whether it was worthwhile to use Zimbabwe dollars in trade. They produced real goods and services out of their time, labour and resources, but were being paid in money that had been created out of nothing.

The state therefore had to enforce more radical and restrictive legal tender laws in order to keep the population using the newly printed money in everyday trade. And in order to stop the inflation effects of money printing, the state turned to price controls. Inevitably, since prices and money affect all aspects of an economy, the state bounded down the path of totalitarian control, forcing people to use the currency and then further forcing the population to keep prices low.

3.3. Raid and plunder

As the authorities became financially desperate, they began violating private property rights by plundering the nation's assets. It became illegal for anyone to hold foreign currency. Exporters, who were managing to do quite well at this stage of the crisis, had to bring all their foreign currency home and deposit it with the Reserve Bank of Zimbabwe at unfavourable rates. Then the Reserve Bank, at the government's behest, raided bank balances by instituting withdrawal limits that severely restricted people's access to money.

Finally, the government turned to Zimbabwe's most crucial and politically sensitive resource: Land.

> *The war veterans invaded the property, locking the farmer and his family in the bathroom for about two days. We had to negotiate for many hours and finally the veterans let the family go – but only after a lot of flattery from my side and free alcohol. That family lost their farm but luckily came away with their lives.*

> – Former head of a Zimbabwean NGO

Land ownership was and still is a highly contentious issue in Zimbabwe. Post-colonial societies grapple with the lingering problem of land justice, and by the turn of the twenty-first century, the land question in Zimbabwe took on a political life of its own. The government began expropriating farmland, allowing war veterans to invade farms as the judiciary largely turned a blind eye. The major part of the productive base of the economy was rendered defunct.

Land politics

The land raids were as much politically motivated as they were economically driven. In 2000, the government issued a new constitution, which had to be approved by a national referendum. When the general consensus on certain issues went against what President Mugabe wanted, he rejected the consultation process outright, rewriting the constitution to include his key points – most notably a *life president* term for himself.

As time came for the referendum, the opposition political party worked closely with the farming community and its tens of thousands of farm workers. This coalition succeeded in a *no vote* against the new constitution. The coalition of the opposition party and farming community were becoming a powerful political bloc. Humiliated by his first electoral defeat, Mugabe reacted strongly, announcing an acceleration of land reform. Days after the referendum, the war veterans began a string of violent farm invasions, and by the middle of that year, the government announced plans for 2 455 farms to be claimed, resettling 150 000 farm families.[10]

The process quickly descended into a brutal and frenzied land grab with most farms being distributed to politically connected officials. Large mobs entered farms by force, kicking farmers off their properties. Almost without exception, the farms were stripped of all assets that could be sold.

The process effectively destroyed the opposition's political networks, but the economic effects were far more devastating. Zimbabwe's agricultural and mining export industries shrivelled away. Farms stopped supplying local markets with food, and a food supply crisis erupted. Those who took over the land had little farming expertise, and the land largely reverted to bare earth and bushveld.

The various industries up and down the agricultural and mining supply chain closed down. These once highly productive industries became a whisper of their former selves.

Farmers who had bank loans simply couldn't repay after their land was taken, so banks stopped accepting land title deeds as collateral, which significantly reduced people's ability to access finance. These defaults on farm loans shook the banking sector to its core. The land reform process wrecked lending markets, making it far more difficult for other non-farm businesses to borrow money. The entire financial sector contracted as private property rights were stripped away from citizens by their government.

Faced with the threat of imminent economic collapse, the government made a short-sighted decision. It turned fully to the only option it had left – printing money to fund all of its expenditures exclusively, leading to the destruction of the currency and the entire economy.

The government's land policies – and the associated collapse of industry – significantly exacerbated the effects of hyperinflation. Other episodes of hyperinflation in other countries have had less severe effects. The extent to which a government will go to maintain expenditures by money printing and thieving private property directly affects the severity of the crisis.

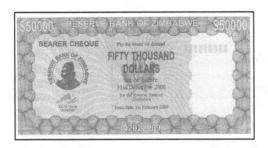

Timing

The economic storm had been building for two decades and began intensifying after Black Friday in 1997. But the torrents of extreme hyperinflation were only seen about a decade later, culminating in the ultimate deluge of rising prices, economic destruction and dollarisation[11] in November 2008. Money printing took time to work its way through the economy with a delayed inflation effect. The rates of money printing grew significantly from 1988 but ballooned after the Black Friday of 1997. The growth in inflation was small at first, but eventually accelerated when people lost confidence in the currency. Following Black Friday, it took 11 years for the currency finally to collapse.

Annual inflation figures for consumer goods in Zimbabwe were staggering, as shown in Table 1:

Date	Rate
1997	20%
1998	48%
1999	57%
2000	55%
2001	112%
2002	199%
2003	599%
2004	133%
2005	586%
2006	1,281%
2007	66 212%
2008 Jul	231 150 888%
2008 Aug	471 000 000 000%
2008 Sep	3 840 000 000 000 000 000%
2008 Mid-Nov	89 700 000 000 000 000 000 000%

Table 1: Annual inflation figures
Source: Hanke, Steve and Kwok, Alex. 'On the Measurement of Zimbabwe's Hyperinflation', *Cato Journal*, Vol. 29, No. 2, Washington DC: Cato Institute, 2009

Storm Warnings in a Nugget

Along the way, the hyperinflationary storm had numerous warning signs that many ignored. The Zimbabwean government lived beyond its means for years, spending more than it could really afford on government programmes, including war and social security. After the Black Friday crash, international lenders pulled back their loans, pushing the country into a debt spiral and multiple market crashes.

The government responded by printing money to fund its expenditures, which it did in ever greater amounts. Simultaneously, it had to increase control over the population and ended up plundering the nation's assets. While this money printing started off as a temporary crisis measure, the authorities found it harder and harder to stop. Money printing gathered momentum and fuelled an inflation frenzy, which poured down economic ruin upon millions of ordinary people. It ultimately led to the Zimbabwe dollar being abandoned as a currency by the end of 2008 – 11 years after Black Friday in 1997.

Zimbabwe's experience is not entirely unique. The path it pursued to hyperinflation has been well trodden by other nations.

Think About It

1. How much debt is your own government in? Can it repay this debt without printing money?

2. If your government wanted to take your land and assets, what would you do?

Chapter 4

Global Money Printing

It is against this background that Government stepped in to save the situation through various interventions by the Reserve Bank of Zimbabwe...

These interventions which were exactly in the mould of bail out packages and quantitative easing measures currently instituted in the US and the EU, were geared at evoking a positive supply response and arrest further economic decline...

Despite numerous intervention measures undertaken by Government through the Reserve Bank of Zimbabwe, economic activity continued to decline progressively with inflation peaking at 231 million percent by July 2008.

> – **Gideon Gono**, governor of the Reserve Bank of Zimbabwe[12]

We had just finished a long interview, and Sarah, a stylish young woman in her mid-twenties, paused for reflection. Her distant gaze was a mixture of colonial charm and reflective nostalgia. And as she reached for her glass, I could tell she was going to make a poignant statement:

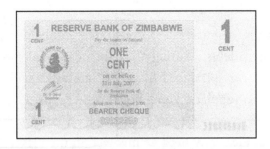

You know, at school we studied the German hyperinflation of the 1920s. I remember thinking at the time: What a bizarre situation – who could possibly live like that?...I would never have imagined that within a few short years we would be living life exactly as the Germans did, replete with wheelbarrows of money and empty stores. How wrong I was.

Yes, how wrong she was! She had come to take for granted the basic things in life.

I, too, studied the German hyperinflation in my high school history class. For the schoolboy me, the story had a macabre surrealism about it. The footage was black and white and seemed to be on constant fast-forward. How on earth could a society get to the stage where people had to carry money packed in a wheelbarrow just to pay for a loaf of bread?

As I studied the Zimbabwean hyperinflation, the German hyperinflation of the 1920s began to make more sense. The precursors to Zimbabwe's hyperinflation were uncannily similar to that of Germany's.

From well before the twentieth century, Germany was an industrial force and had pivotal economic influence throughout Europe. But by the end of 1923, its money was worthless and the majority of its manufacturing base had shut down – impoverishing the nation and ultimately leading to the rise of Adolf Hitler's extreme fascism. The years between 1921 and 1923 are regarded as the years of acute hyperinflation, but Germany's economic storm had actually begun years before. Like Zimbabwe, Germany was saddled with large debts, leading to a financial panic that pushed the country down a debt spiral and finally to the political decision to print money, control the population and violate land rights.

In late July 1914, Germany became involved in the biggest war the world had known. The war was to prove exceptionally expensive and wasteful, catapulting Germany into significant debt. The German government responded by suspending all redemptions of gold for its currency, the mark, and began to print money on a large scale. The war crippled the country's productive base and forced it to run large trade and fiscal deficits to maintain consumption levels and meet social security obligations.

In 1918, after the war, the Allied forces met in Versailles to impose onerous penalties on Germany for its part in the conflict, burdening it with even more financial obligations for its ailing economy. Compounding the harsh terms, Germany was forced to surrender much of its productive land to neighbouring countries.

Impoverished and disempowered, the German government made the political decision to print money to pay its debts and fund expenditures, which finally pushed the country into hyperinflation and the collapse of its currency at the end of 1923.

In total, nine years passed from the start of the war to the final collapse of the German mark.

Do These Principles Still Apply Today?

> The only thing we learn from history is that we learn nothing from history.
>
> – Friedrich Hegel

There are alarming similarities between the precursors to the Zimbabwean and German hyperinflations and present global trends. Governments of highly developed countries have in recent years turned to money printing to solve their financial problems.

The precursors of Zimbabwe's hyperinflation have many fascinating parallels to what we see happening in present-day United States, Britain, the Eurozone and Japan.

1. Running Up Debts

1.1. False promises: large pensions and social security

In the United States, the government has legal obligations to pay social security, medical costs and pensions for retirees. The total amount allocated in the US 2014 budget for general healthcare, Medicare, Income Security, and Social Security was $2.4 trillion. In other words, social security spending consists of over half of the total federal government's annual expenses. The number of welfare recipients grows by nearly 5000 people every day, and this is accelerating as the baby boomer generation begins to retire.[13]

In 1950, there were about ten taxpaying employees for every person receiving some form of social security benefit in America. By 2013, that number reduced to just 1.5 taxpayers for every social security recipient.[14]

Although estimates vary, the total social security liability in the US is estimated to be at least $100 trillion, and some estimates have it at as much as $220 trillion. This means if every family in America had to fund it, they would each have to pay between $1 million and $2.5 million after tax *out of their own pockets*!

The government presently has insufficient assets to pay pensioners – these pension obligations are known as *unfunded liabilities*. Monthly contributions of the existing workforce are used to pay out existing pensions, but there just isn't enough coming in to cover the fast-growing pension liabilities indefinitely. Social security is on a fundamentally unsustainable path and these public pension funds are careering headlong towards a cliff, where they will be unable to pay out pensions.

Japan, Europe and Britain have the same kind of problems, with their ageing populations – who are living longer than ever before – placing unsustainably large demands on their young, productive populations. This adds up to a significant and rising annual expense, eating into resources needed elsewhere in their economies. Compared to the size of their populations, pension and social security obligations are similar in the Eurozone, Britain, Japan and the United States.

The many millions who receive pensions and social security grants represent a large voting bloc with a powerful vested interest in their very livelihood. There is growing pressure on politicians to appease this bloc by making sure the benefits keep flowing at all costs.

Relatively, the small pension that Zimbabwe paid out doesn't even come close in comparison to the massive social security obligations in these major economies.

1.2. Military misadventures

The major NATO allies (including most of the Eurozone, the UK and America) have been involved in an extensive and costly campaign rather vaguely labelled the *War on Terror*. US military expenditures in particular are sky-high and rising. The US government currently spends about 30% of tax revenues, or over $800 billion, every year on running the US military machine. That's double what it spent annually at the turn of the twenty-first century and has an equivalent cost to every American family of about $8 000, every year. America certainly has its fair share of war veteran pension and social security benefits – each year it pays out over $150 billion to war veterans.

Britain, the Eurozone and Japan all have large military budgets, but they pale in comparison to America's, which alone accounts for just under half of the world's total military expenditures.

1.3. Debt sweat: pressure from lenders

The regions with the four major international currencies (US dollar, euro, British pound and Japanese yen) are all deeply indebted. Governments and private households have been living beyond their means for decades.

Excluding welfare obligations, the combined debt of the US government and its household sector at the end of 2013 was approximately US$30 trillion.[15] The US government in particular is heavily reliant on foreign sources of funding. As the Mugabe regime discovered, an addiction to foreign funding is dangerous when foreigners become reluctant to carry on lending.

Here is a summary of government and household debt in the major economies at the start of 2014:[16]

Debt of the major economies compared to tax revenues

Country	Government debt (national, state and local)	Unfunded liabilities (social security)	Total annual government revenue	Total government debt to tax revenue
United States (2014)	US$20 trillion	US$100 trillion	US$4.3 trillion	27x
Japan (2014)	¥1.1 quadrillion	¥1.2 quadrillion	¥140 trillion	16x
United Kingdom (2014)	£1.5 trillion	£5.6 trillion	£580 billion	12x
Eurozone (2014)	€9.2 trillion	€38 trillion	€4.4 trillion	10x
Zimbabwe (1997)	US$5.1 billion	NA	US$2.2 billion	2x

Table 2: Debt of the major economies compared to tax revenues
Sources: *The Economist, Datastream, Federal Reserve, Bloomberg, EuroStat, Statistics Japan, Office of National Statistics (ONS), OECD*

The culture of debt has spread far beyond the halls of government. The United States as a whole, including the government and the private sector, currently imports about US$500 billion more than it exports every year.[17] This means that annually, an American family of four consumes, on average, nearly US$8 000 worth of goods *from* the rest of the world more than it produces *for* the rest of the world, adding to a growing debt that must be repaid at some stage in some way. America must either begin to consume less and pay what it owes, or face a moment when the rest of the world stops funding its consumption. Most of Europe has similar problems. Even

Japan, which used to be a consistent net exporter to the rest of the world, has become a net importer of goods and services.

To put the above numbers into context, if every American tax dollar each year was diverted away from all government departments and *only* used to build up a fund to cover unfunded liabilities and repay the national government debt, it would take about three decades to repay – and that's assuming that *all* other government expenditure stopped immediately and the government completely shut down!

Debts have been rising, placing increasing power in the hands of international lenders. Germany, as the main lender to Europe, has tremendous political authority in the region purely because of its lending strength. Likewise, China and other global lenders such as Middle East oil producers have grown in their financial authority on a global scale as they become primary lenders to the developed economies.

At the same time, within five years after the 2008 financial crisis, the US Federal Reserve doubled its money supply (M1).

The lessons from Zimbabwe are clear. Zimbabwe's government consumed too much and became highly indebted, complacent, and over-reliant on foreign funders, while at the same time increased its money supply in the economy. The government developed an unsustainable spending habit and when the funding suddenly dried up, it was left with two options: either take the hard road and live within its means or bumble down a potholed inflation road leading to destruction.

The major developed economies of the world today face just such challenges. They are living in the *debt sweat*, and some, like Greece, Italy, Spain and Portugal, have come to the brink of outright default. The rising debt of the major countries supports the Rogoff-Reinhart findings we mentioned in Chapter 3. A worldwide government debt and currency crisis remains one of the largest of all global economic risks.

2. Financial Crisis

2.1. Black Friday event

It's no longer in China's favour to accumulate foreign-exchange reserves...

> – Yi Gang, deputy governor of the Chinese central
> bank, highlighting China's reluctance to continue
> lending to America, November 2013[18]

Although the specific details differ, financial crises always have the same complexion – debts build up unsustainably through reckless borrowing and lending until eventually borrowers can't repay, causing a loss of confidence in the banking system, a collapse of lending, and a sharp decline in economic activity.

The banking crisis of 2008 was colossal and international in its reach, tearing through financial systems from Iceland to Dubai and Japan to Ireland. Banks, particularly in the major economies, had lent recklessly to governments, companies, and households. One major area of reckless lending was mortgage lending. When people couldn't repay their home loans, banks started to get into financial trouble. Trust within the global

banking system evaporated, culminating in financial market panic in late 2008 and a prolonged economic slump known as the Great Recession.

To try restore stability and confidence back to the financial system, the major central banks of the world began printing money on a large scale to bail out the commerical banks and indebted governments.

In Zimbabwe, major international lenders, who had lent recklessly to the Zimbabwean government for many years, suddenly stopped lending as they realised Zimbabwe would be unable to repay. On Black Friday – 14 November 1997 – the value of Zimbabwe's currency crashed as confidence in the government and the economy plummeted. The banking system began to seize up, banks became fearful to lend, and economic activity plunged.

With the government going broke and the banks in major trouble, Zimbabwe's central bank began printing money on a large scale to bail them out.

For all the money the world's major economies have printed to date since the 2008 financial crisis, it hasn't yet been enough to spark a wholesale loss of confidence in currencies or runaway hyperinflation. Furthermore, it would be naïve to underestimate the ability of policy makers with enormous vested interests to delay the day of reckoning for their precarious fiscal situation. Yet the 2008 financial crisis has started a trend of money printing and debt spending, the extent of which is likely to lead at some stage to another major financial crisis and loss of confidence in currencies. America and the major economies are yet to have their true Black Friday moment, where lenders permanently withdraw financial support..[19]

McKinsey & Company estimate that the world economy – governments, households, and companies – went a further $57 trillion into debt between 2007 and 2014, with total global debts exceeding $200 trillion, and counting. Governments alone account for nearly half of this increase.[20] A large proportion of this new debt comes from newly printed money lent out by central banks and commercial banks. In other words, instead of reforming the financial and economic system to avoid the mistakes of the past, the major economies of the world have tried to fix their debt problems with even more debt, making the global financial system arguably even more fragile.

It is certain that, if governments continue to pile up debts recklessly and to devalue their currency by printing money, a day of debt reckoning must come.

2.2. Debt spiral

While the ultimate Black Friday moment has not happened yet in the world's major economies, the 2008 financial crisis has been a catalyst to push most developed countries into a slippery government spending and debt spiral. American government debt has grown by a teeth-clattering $8 trillion, up over 80% in the seven years since the crisis – equivalent to an *additional* $67 000 of debt for every American family, and rising. By the end of its terms, the Obama administration will have borrowed more money in eight years than all administrations from Lyndon B Johnson to George W Bush combined,[21] and the same pattern is playing out in the other major economies. Pension debts continue to rise and war expenditures remain.

In Europe, Britain and Japan, the government debt levels also continue to soar.

With the massive amount of debt that the US and other developed economies have accumulated, they will either have to default, print money or increase taxes *significantly* to repay debts. Most likely they will choose some combination of all three.

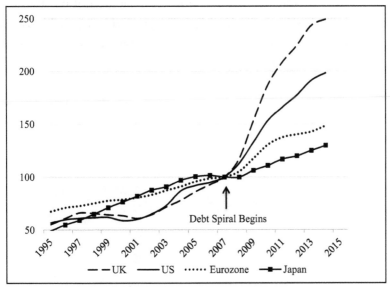

Chart 3: General government debt
Major indebted economies, 1995–2014 (base 100 in 2007)
Source: International Monetary Fund, Eurostat, St Louis Federal
Reserve Bank, Philip Haslam & Russell Lamberti

The debt spiral has begun. The chart below shows how debt burdens in the major industrialised economies have relatively accelerated higher after the global financial crisis.

Chart 3 shows comparative growth rates of debt in each of these economies. However, the absolute debt figures vary in each of these economies. Since 2007, the UK and US have become much more profligate – the US government almost doubled its debt in the time period to 2014, and the UK government increased its debt by almost 2.5 times.

3. The Political Decision

3.1. Money printing
America's response to the financial crisis has been to print money on a large scale via its quantitative easing programmes. Other major economies have done likewise. In 2013, the Federal Reserve printed just over US$1 trillion to bail out the banks and the US government, 40% of all the money it had printed in the previous 100 years.[22]

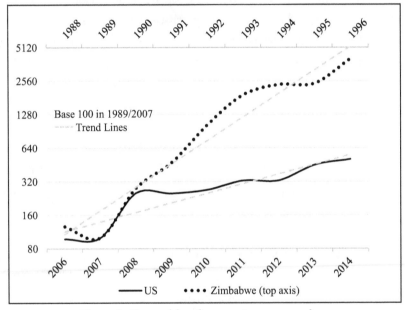

Chart 4: Central bank assets/ monetary base
United States 2006–2014 & Zimbabwe 1988–1996 (log-scale)
Source: International Monetary Fund, St Louis Federal Reserve
Bank, Philip Haslam & Russell Lamberti

Chart 4 illustrates that Zimbabwe's money printing programme was larger than America's, comparatively. However, there is definitely a significant upward trend in US money printing.

For Japan, an economy less than half the size of the United States, the scale of money printing in 2013, relatively, was more than double the size of that of the US! By 2015, the rate of Japanese money printing had escalated 60% to ¥80 trillion created *every year* in order to repay its government debts.

From 2008 to early 2015, the Bank of England printed about £310 billion, the same amount of money printing as America relative to the size of Britain's economy. The European Central Bank had been relatively conservative, printing about €1 trillion over the same period. This has been about 60% as large as America's money printing programme relative to the size of Eurozone GDP. However, in January 2015, the European Central Bank became more aggressive in its plans, announcing that it would begin printing about €60 billion every month to bail out indebted governments and banks.

From September 2008 to early 2015 these four major central banks combined almost printed a staggering US$7 trillion, and counting. This would be roughly enough to purchase all the listed companies in Brazil, Russia, India and China.

In the five years from 2008 to the end of 2013, the Federal Reserve increased the money supply by 4.5 times, printing US$350 for every US$100 it had printed in the previous 100 years, indirectly lending that newly printed money to government and banks.

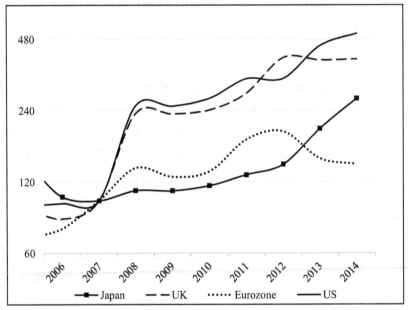

Chart 5: Central bank money printing
Central Bank Assets, 2006–2014 (log-scale, base 100 in 2007)
Source: International Monetary Fund, St Louis Federal Reserve
Bank, Philip Haslam & Russell Lamberti

Each of the major four currency blocs has been significantly increasing their money supply. The effects of this money printing may not be clearly seen in official measures of consumer prices yet, but it is certainly causing price inflation. House prices and stock market prices in particular rose considerably from 2012 to 2015, giving rise to concerns about new financial bubbles. At the same time, as much money as these countries have already printed, the large size of their economies and currency systems means that money printing hasn't yet sparked runaway inflation of the sort that would be associated with hyperinflation. However, with the enormous government debt burdens in America and other developed economies, if leaders continue to make the wrong political decisions, the amount of money currently being printed will only be the tip of the iceberg. These countries are steadily adopting the dangerous policies that ultimately proved disastrous in Zimbabwe.

3.2. Raid and plunder

With escalating government debt burdens in the world's major economies, attempts to raise taxation are increasing in almost every facet of life and the state looms a larger threat over private property rights. Governments across the world are making it increasingly difficult for ordinary citizens to conduct business and acquire and use private property without heavy oversight, regulation and taxation. And as governments struggle with their enormous debts, the incentives to increase taxes are only increasing.

For example, in March 2013, bank customers in Cyprus with deposits larger than €100 000 had their money confiscated to bail out the Cypriot banks. Known as a *bail-in*, unsuspecting depositors had their accounts raided in order to pay for the bank rescue – a blunt confiscation of people's cash.

Alarmingly, the Cyprus model has been proposed for other instances of bank failure in other countries. In December 2013, the European Parliament finalised a directive that allows the authorities to claim bail-ins for bank rescues.[23] The same is being introduced for British[24] and US banks[25] and is being proposed for Canadian banks.[26]

In June 2014, the European Central Bank instituted negative interest rates on commercial bank deposits at the central bank. Commercial banks have to *pay* the central bank to deposit money with it. The Swiss, Swedish

and Danish central banks did the same[27]. The central banks are trying to incentivise banks to lend more money into already heavily indebted economies.

Meanwhile, with many public pension schemes unable to pay out pension benefits fully for much longer, and with limited options available, governments are looking to change the rules. In 2011, the European Central Bank suggested various ways to tackle the unsustainable pensions, including 'imposing new taxes', levying 'additional social contributions' and 'taxing previously untaxed pension benefits'.[28]

Historically, numerous countries that experienced similar problems reduced benefit payouts, in the process defaulting on their contractual obligations to pensioners. Others have turned to the assets of private pension companies, taking them to help pay for the national pension schemes – including recently Ireland, Poland, Hungary, Bulgaria and Argentina.[29]

This happened in Zimbabwe, where the government targeted the very large and wealthy private pension funds as a first source of funding by forcing them to lend more to the government. The response may very well be similar in the major indebted economies.

The land reform process in Zimbabwe, where land was forcibly taken during the hyperinflation years, was unique and had many contributing factors, particularly the residual political problems stemming from colonialism.

The loss of private property rights for land was a significant contributor in obliterating the major productive sector of Zimbabwe's economy and played an especially damaging role in Zimbabwe's hyperinflation. However, the same political and economic factors that led to money printing were at play – too much debt and political pressure to appease disenchanted voters.

While the possibility of Zimbabwe-style land grabs may be remote in most developed economies, another surreptitious form of land nationalisation is taking place. As part of quantitative easing programmes, central banks print money to purchase *mortgage-backed securities*. These are, as the name suggests, ordinary mortgage loans repackaged as tradable securities. Typically these mortgages are backed by properties as collateral. As property owners across the US and Europe foreclose, the central banks that hold these *mortgage-backed securities* effectively acquire the properties backing the foreclosed mortgages (through large associated government organisations)[30]. In effect, quantitative easing facilitates the nationalisation of land.

3.3. State control
Hand in hand with the growing threat of raid and plunder is the rise of state control. In the United States, Japan, Europe and Britain, the centralisation of power into the hands of government has put these authorities in a powerful position to dictate globally how people use money. This is key to retaining power should there be a loss of confidence in their currencies following a sovereign debt crisis and a larger scale money printing programme. We discuss this in more detail in chapters 6 and 11.

Timing

How long will the effects of these vast money printing programmes take to work through the global financial system? This isn't an easy question to answer. After Black Friday, it took 11 years for the Zimbabwe dollar to collapse. The German mark collapsed nine years after the major printing

programme started. It would, however, be foolish to use this as a simplistic guideline for other nations. Many hyperinflationary episodes of the past have developed much quicker (some from as little as four years) and some took longer to develop. Zimbabwe's economic mismanagement and money printing schemes can be traced back to the 1980s, even though its crisis moment only appeared in 1997 and its final currency collapse in 2008.

There are numerous other factors that affect the timing of a hyperinflationary spiral. The size of government debts always plays a major role and whether those debts are denominated in local or foreign currency. The pace and relative amount of money being printed is important, as is the makeup of the country's lenders – locals or foreigners. How and where newly printed money is used is an important factor. Government regulation can certainly worsen the effects of hyperinflation. Political systems, the decisions of leaders, public confidence in the ruling authorities, investor psychology, and financial sector sophistication are just some of the key factors that play a role in determining the speed and intensity with which a country can descend into hyperinflation.

Money printing over time creates cultural changes in an economy and the timing of these cultural responses is unique to any situation. The important lesson from Zimbabwe and other hyperinflations is that the effects of high indebtedness and money printing can be masked for long periods of time while they grow in cumulative momentum, eventually producing irresistibly negative consequences.

Global Money Printing in a Nugget

Like Zimbabwe, the industrialised countries are turning to money printing to revive their ailing economies. While the amounts of new money being printed are staggering, they have not yet been enough to spark runaway inflation. Nonetheless, these economies are adopting dangerous policies that history has shown are hard to reverse. High levels of government debt and money printing to supplement government's spending habits, if continued unchecked, will lead to a currency crisis that either ends in a painful debt default or in an even more painful hyperinflation.

Political leaders need to make tough choices in the years ahead – choices that leaders in Germany after World War I, in Zimbabwe during the 1990s and in many other nations in history failed to make. These choices entail economic pain and will risk political leaders' popularity. It will be the mark of great leaders if they can make the hard choices that can avert the worst-case outcome: a hyperinflationary disaster.

It will be easier to keep printing money. It always is.

Think About It

1. Are there similarities between your country's economy and Zimbabwe's, prior to its currency collapse?

2. Does your government rely heavily on foreign lenders to fund its expenditures?

Chapter 5

Hyperinflation 101

Continued inflation inevitably leads to catastrophe.

– Ludwig von Mises

We had just finished breakfast, and my brother told me a story that both shocked and fascinated me. He had taken a hot-air balloon ride on his recent trip to Egypt and was recounting how the same Egyptian tour company had experienced a fatal crash a few months later in February 2013.

The day began routinely with 20 eager tourists climbing into the small balloon basket to enjoy the breathtaking aerial views over the ancient landscape. The temple of Karnak lay in the distance, with the Valley of the Kings in the foreground split by the winding Nile River. Luxor, an old town 700 kilometres south of Cairo, is steeped in history, and the balloon ride was an extremely popular 'must-see' tourist attraction.

The balloon was returning to land after its early morning sightseeing trip. The pilot and ground crew were navigating to the landing site when, just 2 metres above the ground, one of the four gas cylinders sprung a leak and burst into flames. The pilot, who was close to the cylinder, was doused in the blaze, and he leapt out the carriage in a state of panic.

With one fewer passenger, the balloon was suddenly lighter, and the additional heat from the fire created an upward pull, causing the balloon to rise. Everyone was focused on the burning cylinder, and in the confusion of the moment, few noticed the increasing altitude. One alert British passenger realised what was happening and jumped through the flames to the safety of the ground below. With two fewer passengers and the flames burning hotter, the balloon began to rise faster.

As the ill-fated balloon climbed, seven people jumped out, some doing so even at a height of 100 metres. By that time, it was too late – the leaping passengers jumped to their end. As each person jumped, the balloon had less weight pulling it down, and it accelerated into the sky.

The fire now burned searingly hot as the balloon rose to about a kilometre above the earth. Soon the fire engulfed the full canopy of the balloon and consumed its nylon covering. The moment the balloon lining disintegrated, the upward pull ceased. Another gas cylinder burst, and the remains of the balloon and carriage fell out of the sky, crashing to the ground in a nearby field below. On impact, the last of the gas cylinders exploded.[31]

*   *   *

When I heard this horrific story, I was documenting my research on the events in Zimbabwe and pondering how to describe what I had discovered – particularly how to explain hyperinflation in an analogy. As I listened to my brother relate the story of the hot-air balloon, it occurred to me that money printing has the same chilling consequences. This sad story powerfully parallels the course of Zimbabwe's hyperinflation.

Once the Zimbabwean government had given itself over to money printing, it lost control. The fires of money printing burned and national prices rose, leaving millions in a precarious position. Prices accelerated upward

at an extreme rate and eventually reached a point where no price was great enough. At that moment, the currency collapsed, falling to the ground in a blaze of hyperinflation. Ordinary Zimbabweans lost everything and many fled the country. The start was slow – almost unnoticeable. But the effects at the end were catastrophic.

> *Few people can understand hyperinflation without living through it.*
> *It isn't a dry topic to be studied by academics. It affected everyone.*
> *Even the taxi drivers in Zimbabwe could tell you about the details of*
> *hyperinflation. The issues became so obvious when you lived through it.*

> – Zimbabwean economic commentator

What is Hyperinflation?

Hyperinflation, simply explained, is extreme price inflation. Often referred to just as 'inflation', price inflation is a general increase in prices in the economy. Hyperinflation is essentially a period of economic chaos when confidence in the currency deteriorates markedly, leading to a rapid, chaotic, and uncontrollable rise in the prices of goods and services, and the eventual collapse of confidence in the currency.

In formal academic literature, many economists try to pinpoint the rate of inflation that reveals when a country has definitively entered hyperinflation, but opinions vary wildly, from 100% to 12 874% per year.[32] The specific thresholds are arbitrary and misleading. Practically speaking, hyperinflation isn't a measured rate. It is a set of *cultural states*.

As a field for economic study, it is better to look at the critical *qualitative* changes in an economy, rather than randomly selected *quantitative* thresholds. These cultural changes are much more nuanced and yet have much better usefulness in describing the path of hyperinflation and analysing those countries that have gone down this path. Hence, this study has focused far more on these qualitative aspects of hyperinflation.

A leading economist in Zimbabwe, Jonathan Waters, said it this way during my interview with him:

> *Exact inflation becomes meaningless. Hyperinflation is more a sense of being than specific rates. In Zimbabwe no one thought in percentage inflation. You just got a feel for it – you knew the rate on any day in a very intangible way. It was the topic at every dinner table and we talked about it all the time. There were many indicators that you could apply but none was definitive. Knowing the true rate was more of a sensory ability.*

In fact, hyperinflation is never a *moment*. It is a collection of many critical points – a process. And while it has to do with prices rising, *it is really the dramatic process of an established currency losing its usefulness as money*. Each stage of this process inflicts pain on the lives of communities in unique and debilitating ways, which together combine to form the dramatic process of hyperinflation. Based on the numerous interviews of Zimbabweans from all walks of life, we have built a framework to understand these multiple hyperinflation stages.

However, to understand hyperinflation, one needs to understand inflation first. And to understand inflation, one needs to understand prices.

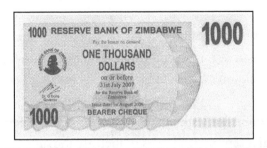

Prices and Inflation

Prices are crucial signals. They direct all economic activity, coordinating the actions of millions of buyers, sellers and producers. Almost everything you possess or use is associated with a price: your salary, the food you eat, the place you live in. Interest rates and stock market values are prices. Anything traded between a buyer and seller has a price. Even free stuff has a price – *someone* had to pay for it!

Without prices, we wouldn't be able to make informed trading decisions. Prices tell us whether something is worth purchasing or not, according to our preferences. And they send signals to suppliers of goods and services to help them decide if something is worth supplying. All economic activity revolves around this simple concept of prices.

Dictionary.com defines inflation as:

> *A persistent and substantial rise in the general level of prices, related to an increase in the volume of money and resulting in the loss of value of currency.*

Inflation is most often caused by an increase in money in an economy. As newly printed money made its way around Zimbabwe, people had more money to buy the products they needed, causing prices to rise.

Some economists think that increasing the amount of money, and therefore increasing market prices, is a good thing. The truth is that printing money sets in motion insidious, highly destructive forces.

Pro-inflation economists argue that since additional money causes prices to increase, a signal is sent to producers to increase the supply of goods. People are employed, equipment is purchased and the economy is 'stimulated'. The argument sounds compelling, and yet it is greatly misleading.

New money is always injected into a specific area of an economy. When this happens, prices rise in those sectors, making business opportunities there *seem* attractive – it makes those sectors look like they are more profitable than they really are. Soon the new money ripples out into the rest of the economy, and prices everywhere begin to rise. Without a continued inflow of new money, the stimulated sectors are revealed to be no more profitable than they were before the injection. Entrepreneurs who invested in these sectors hoping for good profits find that many of these ventures fall flat. Real resources have been wasted. The inflation caused by new money printing created misleading signals. The increased prices were attractive to suppliers, but they were tricked because costs also rose with inflation. Supplier margins weren't any better off.

This process of fooling suppliers into thinking they should supply more goods to specific sectors when it is not as profitable as they expect is called *misallocation of capital*.[33] The initial inflation stimulates certain sectors of the economy, but without continually increasing the amount of money to that sector (fooling suppliers on a repeated basis), a slump in activity follows. The boom is unsustainable and false. The economy needs to readjust and soon after the initial false boom, a depression follows.

In the initial phases of money printing, the areas of the economy that repeatedly get new money begin to grow relative to the rest of the economy.

These areas of the economy begin to experience a large and prolonged misallocation of capital, preceding a greater and more destructive depression and economic adjustment, which is inevitable when the flow of new money eventually stops. This is one of the reasons that banks and companies close to the banking sector tend to be more prosperous in economies with central banks.

Money Printing Gives Government Great Power

Both those who control money printing and those who receive that money first are in a powerful position. If an unrestrained government decides to use its money printing privilege as a way to pay for its expenses, it can spend with limited direct accountability. It can manipulate how markets naturally and organically operate. And it can purchase real goods and services with newly printed money, acquiring more and more for itself at the expense of those who don't have the special privilege of printing money.

If money is printed on an ongoing basis, inflation becomes a culturally accepted norm. In modern society, ask anyone if they think prices will be higher next year, and you'll get only one answer: *Of course.*

Inflation Makes People Poorer

The daily expenses of those who do not receive newly printed money early in the inflation process tend, on average, to rise faster than incomes. Money printing may appear to increase the amount of activity in an economy, but stealthily it makes economic conditions more difficult – most people find themselves worse off than before. The higher the rate of money printing and inflation, the worse off people generally are. In short, inflation makes people poorer by stealing their purchasing power.

*　　*　　*

Inflation Waterfalls: The Six Gorge Moments of Hyperinflation

A few years back, I hiked down a deep ravine cut into South Africa's Hottentots-Holland mountains, known locally as Suicide Gorge. It is interspersed by a series of perilous waterfalls – you can only get down by jumping down each waterfall. As I leapt from the top of the cliff to the first deep pool below, I realised there was no turning back. Once you start a journey down Suicide Gorge, you're pretty much committed. The only way out of the gorge is to continue through it, leaping off ever larger, surging waterfalls into smaller and shallower pools.

In many senses, it is similar travelling down the path of hyperinflation. Reckless money printing sends an economy floundering down a raging ravine of hyperinflation towards economic disaster – there's only one way out, and that's down the gorge. Zimbabwe had six definitive cultural changes in its economy. We call these Gorge Moments – critical 'waterfalls' in the torrent of money printing that propelled the society towards ever greater disaster.

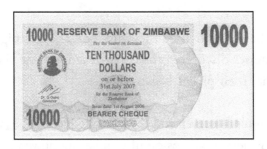

Gorge Moment 1: Past Inflation Becomes Future Inflation

Prices, in the early stage of an inflation, usually rise by less than the increase in the money supply, but in the later stage of an inflation always rise by more than the increase in the money supply.

> — **Henry Hazlitt**, What You Should Know About
> Inflation

In my brother's hot-air balloon story, the passengers looked over the side of the carriage and realised they'd lost the precious moments to jump. Their thoughts, initially concerned about the rising altitude, may have been, *Oh no! If I had jumped then it would have been safer. Now it's higher!* They probably reached a point where it dawned on them that the risks would be far greater seconds later if they *didn't* jump. They may have stopped thinking about past increases in altitude and considered impending future increases in altitude.

Once inflation becomes a culturally accepted norm, people begin adapting their expectations of future price increases based on historic inflation rates. Most likely, you do the same. When you get an increase in salary, or you calculate the price increases for your products, you typically refer to the most recent historic inflation data.

In Zimbabwe, as money was printed at an accelerating rate, many found that they hadn't made sufficient funds available in their budget to make ends meet. Others found that they did not ask for big enough wage increases. Businesses discovered that their revenues rose slower than their expenses and that their profits began to fall.

People are not fooled forever and local Zimbabweans began to catch on, wising up to this perpetual erosion of purchasing power. A critical culture shift began to take place. Instead of calculating price increases on *last year's* inflation, people began to calculate price increases on what they expected inflation to be in the *future*.

This was a crucial turning point. The first cycle of inflation started off with increased amounts of money and ended with increased prices. Now prices began to rise *before* new money was printed. Prices were driven higher by *expectations* of future price increases, rather than by past money printing.

As everyone increased prices, those who were in weaker positions to raise prices or make wage demands were especially hurt in this phase. Pensioners, for instance, were on fixed incomes whose increases were only reviewed annually and based on past inflation rates. The companies most affected by this were those at the end of the supply chain who couldn't raise prices as fast as the others – first retailers and then manufacturers. Their costs rose much faster than their selling prices.

Gorge Moment 2: Money Shortages

The Reserve Bank of Zimbabwe was printing so much money but there wasn't enough money in the economy. They just couldn't keep up with price increases.

> – Managing director of a manufacturing company in Zimbabwe

After Gorge Moment 1, the economy rapidly swept towards a curious and jolting second Gorge Moment. Inflation began to outpace the rate of new money printing and because of the price increases, there was simply not enough money in the economy for everyone to go on purchasing as many goods and services as they had before. Paradoxically, as people raised prices and wage demands, there was not enough money to satisfy these increases. A very strange economic paradox was revealed in Gorge Moment 2: money printing led to shortages of money!

The government now faced an important decision. It could either stop supplying more money into the economy, in which case there would have been a much-needed but extremely painful depression as prices fell, or it could increase the supply of money at an even faster rate than before to match the increases in prices. Naturally, the authorities decided to increase the supply of money.

The first of the major money shortages occurred in 2003 and it led quickly to a run on the banks: queues developed at ATMs as people everywhere lined up to withdraw their savings. They knew that there wasn't enough money to go around and everyone wanted to ensure that their savings were safe. A market quickly developed with a 30% premium being charged for cash in hand relative to cash in the bank. The Reserve Bank of Zimbabwe responded by instituting daily withdrawal limits, which only served to exacerbate growing scepticism with banks.

As people's trust in the banks withered, the money shortages had the unusual effect of encouraging cash-based trade, which only worsened money shortages and pressure on the banks.

Gorge Moment 3: Empty Shops

The shops emptied and supply chains closed down. In their place stepped the dealers and traders. Those who could increase prices the fastest, won.

        – Operations manager of a tannery in Zimbabwe

The very nature of business went through a critical change as Gorge Moment 3 hit. Many companies found their revenues insufficient to pay for subsequent stock purchases. Prices were rising so quickly that the cost of replacing stock was more expensive than the revenue from previous sales. Businesses became fundamentally unsustainable. As real business margins evaporated and profits turned into losses, businesses started to go bankrupt. Most stores did what they could to survive, but the difficulties experienced by increasing inflation ensured that by 2006 practically all stores had closed.

The ability to reduce lead times in supply became a critical competitive advantage in business. Manufacturing processes that required time and patience disappeared. Local production ceased and had to be replaced by imports. Zimbabwe became a *consuming* economy rather than a *producing* economy.

At this juncture, as businesses were shutting down, people and companies switched whatever it was that they normally did to become hoarders, traders and speculators – whatever it took to survive. The entire character of business changed from serving customers to looking out for oneself.

Those in advantaged positions could still game the system, making a quick handling fee, or buy assets and foreign currency.

Gorge Moment 3 threw formal supply chains into disarray, as prices at the point of sale did not compensate companies for the increased cost of their later purchases. Most companies either went bankrupt or attempted to stay afloat by moving into another line of business. The hardest hit were retailers and manufacturers who all had lengthy delivery lead times. Manufacturing for local customers ground to a halt, and stores everywhere emptied as the formal distribution networks shut down. The economy rapidly 'deindustrialised' as companies shut down, mothballed machinery and moved productive businesses offshore. People couldn't get food and goods from shops because the shelves were empty. Prices hurtled higher as a result of an even greater scarcity of goods and services.

The winner-takes-all frenzy in hyperinflation was similar to how I once shared a drink with my brother when we were much younger. We couldn't pour the soda out into separate cups, so he suggested we get two straws and drink it at the same time.

It started out innocently enough, but when I got the feeling that he was drinking more than his fair share, I began to suck harder. He noticed and did the same, which only spurred me to suck even harder. What started off as a brotherly sharing of a drink ended up in a feverish down-down competition with soda fizzing out of our noses and enough burp for an entire afternoon!

Our soda-drinking rivalry illustrates the kind of crazed survival competition that took place between members of society in Zimbabwe's hyperinflation. As personal livelihoods were at stake, trading became nasty.

Gorge Moment 4: The End of Lend

Almost every hyperinflation ends with a class of borrowers who profit from the entire currency collapse like profiteers or thieves.

> – Zimbabwean-born economist based in South
> Africa

Following the business crisis, a banking crisis emerged: Gorge Moment 4. This was the moment that truly ground economic activity to a halt.

It became pointless to save money in the bank, or to lend it, because the value of loans and bank deposits shrank with hyperinflation. Those who had money dared not lend it. They needed to spend it on something – *anything* – that held value longer than the money would.

Banks stopped lending money. They couldn't be sure that the interest they charged would compensate for the rate of inflation. Interest rates for deposits went up to 8000% – those who deposited their money could multiply it 80 times in a year...but this wasn't nearly enough. Many didn't understand what was happening and, attracted by what seemed to be exceptionally high interest rates, naively deposited their savings in the banks. They lost everything.

At Gorge Moment 4, banks realised that the cash reserves they had been accumulating from money printing bailouts were fast losing value with the

high levels of inflation. This was dead money for banks. Since the official interest rates that they were forced to charge couldn't compensate for the loss of value of the loans from inflation, it didn't make sense for banks to lend money out. The banks had the power to create an amount of digital credit money that was many times largerthan the amount of physical notes and coin they had on hand. This placed them in a powerful position. Not only did they reduce lending and accept newly printed money as a bailout, but they increasingly speculated by creating vast amounts of credit money and purchasing assets that would hold their value, such as shares on the stock exchange.

The End of Lend Gorge Moment saw banks (like all other businesses) moving away from their normal trade of deposits and loans to one of using their unique privilege of receiving newly printed cash and creating credit money to speculate, trade and hoard real assets. This only served to accelerate the growing inflation.

The government tried to force the banks to lend, regardless of whether it was profitable or not. The politically connected became the only ones who could get bank loans, which they exploited as a way of profiting from hyperinflation: borrow money and immediately use it to purchase something that would increase in price with inflation, like cars or shares on the stock market.

With companies making significant losses and now unable to borrow, business operations came to a standstill.

Gorge Moment 5: The Flight to Real Value

By 2007, the value of money was eroding on a daily basis. People tried to get rid of it as fast as they could. Money became like a searing hot coal – what we call *scorched money*. When anyone received money, they ran to buy anything they could find as fast as they could. The velocity of money – the frequency with which it changed hands – became frenetic. The economy at this point entered what the Austrian economist Ludwig von Mises called *Katastrophenhausse* – a *doomed boom*. As confidence in money's purchasing power plummeted, everyone tried to get rid of it as fast as possible. This meant a huge demand for goods and services that had the appearance of a boom as prices rose rapidly. But it was actually a full-scale economic collapse, as production collapsed and goods were rapidly consumed, hurtling the economy towards a final disaster.[34]

At Gorge Moment 5, faith in the currency died. The only things keeping the Zimbabwe dollar from outright death at this point were legal tender laws and government force – a force that had to increase in reach and ferocity as the value of money deteriorated. At this stage, no one wanted to hold money – people bought goods and services just to acquire something that would retain its value, if only for a little longer than the money did. Even milk was a better store of value than money!

The whole economy developed a consumption hysteria. Shelves cleared. In addition to buying things that could last (like tools and household goods), people spent money on fleeting experiences, like a game of golf with friends. If you had extra savings, you spent it on anything – much of which ended up perishing. Everything that could be consumed was consumed, and as consumption soared, production evaporated.

Gorge Moment 5 triggered a colossal inflation spiral as price increases accelerated dramatically and the economy became gripped firmly in the death throes of hyperinflation. From here, there was only one direction that the currency could go and that was to an ultimate collapse two years later.

Gorge Moment 6: When Money Dies

The sixth and final Gorge Moment was when the currency could not be maintained by government force any longer, and it crashed out of use. Even the government gave up trading in the money any longer. The final destruction of the Zimbabwe dollar started in November 2008, a process that finally ended in February 2009. Money printing became so endemic and the rise in prices so out of control that no one would use the currency regardless of the pressure from the government.

Technically, inflation rose to infinity as the value of the currency fell to zero. No price was high enough for people to accept payment in Zimbabwe dollars – they just refused to take it.

This Gorge Moment was known as *dollarisation* because one of the stable alternative currencies Zimbabwe adopted at the time was the US dollar. The British pound, South African rand and other currencies were also acceptable as legal tender. At this stage, the Reserve Bank of Zimbabwe surrendered its privileged right to print money.

Up to this point a number of businesses had survived by focusing on exports. Those businesses had experienced the best of both worlds – they received income in comparatively stable foreign currencies that appreciated against the Zimbabwe dollar, and yet they paid expenses in a currency that was collapsing. Before dollarisation, exporters were extremely profitable. They were so profitable that they didn't have to monitor their expenses (and indeed couldn't do so because the accounting numbers changed so quickly with inflation).

But at the moment of dollarisation, almost all export companies collapsed. Suddenly, they had to pay all local expenses in foreign currency. No longer were these local expenses miniscule relative to incomes – now companies had to pay their workers and suppliers in US dollars. Moreover, at dollarisation, many we interviewed told how the Reserve Bank of Zimbabwe simply expropriated most of the remaining foreign currency owned by the exporters.

Most local businesses had shut down during hyperinflation, and now, during dollarisation, almost all export businesses also shut down. The economy went through its last and inevitable contraction – a money reset. No exports meant no foreign currency, and no dollars meant no imports of crucial supplies.

A complete turnaround occurred. People had tried to get rid of their *scorched* Zimbabwe dollars by buying anything they could get their hands on, and now those who had US dollars tried their hardest not to spend them!

There were other jolting effects of dollarisation as well. During the hyperinflation years, there had arisen intricate community supply networks, around which most people derived some form of trading income. The whole barter economy had scores of dealers to facilitate it. Dollarisation

caused this entire supply network to fall away because normal distribution to stores resumed. All those dealers who'd generated income in alternative, non-orthodox supply channels abruptly stopped making money.

With the formal sector destroyed and most of the skilled entrepreneurs, artisans and professionals having left during hyperinflation, most products had to be imported at a high cost – only increasing the local cost of goods in US dollar terms.

Other curious effects of Gorge Moment 6

The Zimbabwe dollar was dead, but inflation expectations hadn't gone away. People had become so used to daily price increases that this continued for a while in US dollars. Businesses that re-emerged now had to deal with the problem of rising prices again – but this time in US dollars.

One executive of a large company said this about dollarisation:

> *Hyperinflation had created terrible expectations for price increases in everyone. After dollarisation, we used a stable currency so we reasonably should have had a low level of inflation. However, our staff were adamant that they needed proper price increases – the concept of a 'once- yearly' increase is only now, after four years, beginning to be accepted.*

We deadlocked in all of our negotiations with the trade unions. They had wanted a 500% inflation increase. We eventually went to arbitration on it, but even the arbitrators didn't understand. They sided with the unions. We're now suing the arbitrators for incompetence.

Since US dollars had to be brought in physically from the United States and other countries, the cost of bringing in US coins was prohibitive. In daily trade, however, cents are typically important for small-value transactions. Retail stores couldn't give small change for purchases, so they would keep a stock of small value items at the tills so that shoppers could 'top-up' at the end of their purchases, to a round number of dollars.

With the lingering culture of inflation, the economy experienced continued shortages of dollars for some time, putting tremendous pressure on businesses after dollarisation. US dollar notes were imported and exchanged tens of thousands of times without going back into the US dollar banking system, making them dirty and barely recognisable. The ruined notes added further significant problems to the dollar shortages.

But now, the government couldn't print more money to alleviate the money shortages temporarily. Instead the cash shortages forced businesses to reduce prices and workers to make wage demands.

The economy came to an almost complete standstill in the early stages of dollarisation. Some economists say that between 75% and 90% of the population were unemployed after years of money printing and the final standstill of the economy. However, to view the transition to dollarisation as a negative transition would be a mistake. It certainly entailed acute short-term pain for the economy, which had become used to functioning in a particular and very peculiar way. But it was vital and inevitable; painful but necessary. It was the only way to get the economy back to a semblance

of normalcy and to correct the gaping market imbalances that had built up around unstable and unsound money.

Hyperinflation 101 in a Nugget

Zimbabwe's hyperinflation was similar to the Luxor hot-air balloon crash. The fires of money printing pushed the rising balloon of prices ever higher, until it eventually consumed the economy with the currency eventually burning out and crashing to the ground, out of use.

Hyperinflation is excessive price inflation caused by unrestrained money printing. Prices rise as a result of this new money, which flows into different sectors and causes a misallocation of capital. This leads to a short-lived boom followed by a destructive depression.

Governments can use money printing to purchase real goods and services and manipulate markets, stimulating some industries over others in the short term. However, they have to resort to increasing money printing to delay the inevitable consequences.

Zimbabwe experienced six Gorge Moments down its path of hyperinflation. Perennial money printing led to a *culture* of inflation in which everyone expected prices to rise in the future. A culture shift occurred as businesses and employees started to raise prices and wage demands respectively, based on expected future inflation rather than historic inflation – Gorge Moment 1. Prices then began to rise faster than the supply of money, leading to the money shortages of Gorge Moment 2.

Gorge Moment 3 hit as profits turned into losses and businesses went bankrupt. Shops emptied, and manufacturing for local customers stopped. Prices rose even faster because of the shortages of real goods and services, and the vicious cycle went around again and again, getting worse each time. The banks stopped lending at Gorge Moment 4, except to the politically connected elite to whom they were forced to lend.

At Gorge Moment 5, fewer and fewer people continued trading in the currency and only did so because of legal tender laws and extreme government force. This pushed the economy into a hyperinflation spiral and led to a consumption of all savings.

Gorge Moment 6 came when the currency collapsed and the government was officially and totally bankrupt. The US dollar became the alternative, stable currency – among other currencies, such as the South African rand and British pound. Export companies closed and dealers went out of business as existing supply networks changed drastically. Economic activity came to its final and inevitable standstill as the last flames of the inflationary mania were extinguished.

Hyperinflation in Zimbabwe was the ultimate in economic chaos and disorder. It destroyed livelihoods and lives, and left in its path economic ruin. Zimbabwe has been forced to rebuild its economy, and indeed its very society, from ground zero. The toll of human suffering was immense. Communities, neighbourhoods and families were torn apart. Living standards plummeted. Basic services disintegrated.

It's really hard to remember the difficult times – I've blocked it out.
I'm not sure I want to remember. By the end it got so bad.

— Zimbabwean now living in South Africa

Think About It

1. Is your government relying on increasing amounts of money printing to 'fix' the economy?

2. Do you find people working harder and harder but being able to afford fewer and fewer everyday goods and services?

3. Do inflation-linked pay increases really compensate for the rising prices of the goods you buy?

4. How would you access money if you couldn't withdraw it from your bank?

Chapter 6

The Politics of Printed Money

The way to crush the bourgeoisie is to grind them between the millstones of taxation and inflation.

– Vladimir Lenin

The dynamics of government control in hyperinflation can be likened to a *Monopoly* game.

A critical component of the game is that one of the players has to be the banker – a player who acts like all the other players, although he is also responsible for the 'new' money coming out the money box. When the players move past GO or redeem cards, they can get money directly from the money box. As this happens, prices of land, houses and hotels tend to rise.

One wintry day in December, some friends gather to play the game in downtown New York at Chete Frawd's apartment. Chete grew up on the shady side of the street and is a con-artist supremo. He has enough grease to keep a train running!

A serial game cheater, Chete convinces his friends that he should be voted in as the banker because he is the host. Early in the game, he begins to sneak money out the money box and uses it during his turn. It isn't much initially, and because he does it sneakily, the other players don't notice. As the game progresses, the ones who started out strong soon begin to go bankrupt.

Chete controls the game with the money he takes from the box. A good friend of his, Rich Banker, colludes with Chete, and because Rich helps him beat the others, Chete also gives him new money out the box. The game fundamentally shifts and becomes unfair for the other players, who begin to lose more than they win, and eventually stop winning altogether. Onist Citsen begins to suspect that Chete is up to no good and openly accuses him, which alerts the other players and makes them resentful.

They either want to stop playing the game or they want another banker who would be fair with the money box. Chete realises that he's been found out, and since he is a bit of a bully, he throws a tantrum to intimidate the other players. He resorts to increasing levels of manipulation to keep things going his way. He locks the door and *demands* that they play the game with him. He, and he alone, will be the banker.

By now, all the other players want to leave. Chete is faced with the dilemma that if he still wants them to play the game, he needs to threaten and control his friends using more and more drastic and aggressive measures.

This is very similar to what happens when governments use the central bank and its money printing press to cheat the system.

Central banks and commercial banks are structured to print money continually. A key to political power lies in the control of this money printing machine, which is why most governments have a major influence on the policies of the central bank and heavily regulate the commercial banks. They get to rig the game in their favour.

The government exerts control in hyperinflation with a steady increase of new money, giving it the power to manipulate markets. It then has to set up an intricate system of legislation, policing, price control and checks on the black market to control daily trade and ensure that people use its printed money.

Zimbabwe's Monopoly Money

By a continuing process of inflation, government can confiscate, secretly and unobserved, an important part of the wealth of their citizens.

– **John Maynard Keynes**, the most famous
economist of the twentieth century

Central banks, it is argued, should be independent institutions from governments. The theory is that governments shouldn't be able to interfere with the nation's currency and manipulate it for its own ends. In practice this is rarely, if ever, true. All governments have at least some control over the important levers of the central bank and usually get to appoint key staff. In most countries commercial banks also have a strong say in how the central bank is run and how much money it prints, although this is not usually explicitly acknowledged. In short, the alliance between governments and banks is fostered and managed by the central bank.

Central bank independence breaks down when governments use it to make money cheaply available for pet projects or to print money to pay off government debts. Typically, when highly indebted governments face a debt crisis, central bank independence is immediately withdrawn. It is an illusory independence – a show of a separation of roles that can be suspended when governments decide to.

In Zimbabwe, the independence between the central bank and the government broke down totally after the Black Friday crash of 1997. The Reserve Bank of Zimbabwe began to operate as an arm of the government and ended up printing whenever the government needed more money.

In an attempt to source foreign currency for the government, the Reserve Bank forced exporters to sell a quarter of all foreign earnings to the government in return for rapidly depreciating Zimbabwe dollars at grossly unfavourable exchange rates. This was an effective tax.

To add to this tax on the foreign currency, when the government's needs demanded it, the Reserve Bank often simply took the balance of foreign earnings from exporters when they ran out of alternatives – outright theft in the name of 'economic policy'.

How Did Money Get to the Streets?

As the Zimbabwean government turned to money printing to fund its expenditures, there were a handful of ways that money made its way to the street. It started off fairly innocuously through 'conventional' channels but became more brazen and overt as time went on.

1. 'Ordinary' central banking practice

In the conventional system, banks create money out of nothing (credit money) and lend it directly to the government by buying government bonds and simply crediting electronic digits to the government bank account. They then use these bonds as security to get newly printed cash from the central bank in order to have just enough in their vaults to facilitate customer cash withdrawals and satisfy financial regulations.

As the economic crisis in Zimbabwe unfolded, it no longer made sense for the banks to lend to the government because the government was going bankrupt. Also, with inflation rampant, by the time bank loans had been repaid, they had lost much of their purchasing power. Meanwhile, bank customers, fearing that their money was becoming worthless, withdrew their deposits. Large-scale cash withdrawals were the worst possible scenario for the banks since they, like all modern banks the world over, had kept only a fraction of the money recorded in their books. They were under severe pressure from both depositors, who were withdrawing money, and the insatiable government, who was constantly borrowing more money.

Banks needed cash desperately and appealed to the Reserve Bank for alternative ways to get newly printed money.

2. Banks withdrawing directly from the Reserve Bank

The Reserve Bank of Zimbabwe therefore changed the rules. It decided to give each bank a direct account – an effective credit card facility with the Reserve Bank with no credit limit. They didn't own a physical credit card, but the facility operated in exactly the same way. Banks could withdraw as much as they wanted at any stage, as they needed.

This process started from as early as 2001. The banks would arrive at 7 a.m. at the Reserve Bank every morning to pick up newly printed cash for their net demands of the day. By 2007, each bank was making three withdrawals a day at allotted times from distribution points known as 'cash depots'.

Realising that the Reserve Bank would make good on any cash shortages, the banks began to speculate in the stock market with the new cash they received, taking advantage of their ability to do real-time transfers and quickly exploiting rising prices. Technically, this was illegal in terms of the Banks Act, but Reserve Bank officials turned a blind eye. The authorities were far more concerned that troubled banks responded in a 'creative' way to stay afloat, even if their activities were illegal.

3. Government hunger for foreign currency – trading directly on the street

The government demand for foreign exchange grew rapidly. It had huge import requirements. State-owned companies needed supplies from offshore. Robert Mugabe's lavish trips abroad had to be funded and other government activities needed forex, such as importing tractors or obtaining antiretroviral drugs for those who were sick with HIV.

Foreign currency became scarce with exports dwindling. No one outside of the country would accept Zimbabwe dollars in exchange for foreign currency, making it difficult to import goods. As businesses closed down, more products had to be imported, which increased the demand for foreign currency. Every month, the government gave the Reserve Bank a specific 'import requirement', and it had to find enough foreign exchange to pay for these imports and foreign expenses.

The Reserve Bank therefore set up a system to sell its newly printed Zimbabwe dollars on the street using people called 'runners'. Each of these street dealers was given massive wads of freshly printed Zimbabwe dollar notes in bags, suitcases and trunks with instructions to buy a certain amount of foreign currency. The Reserve Bank didn't necessarily care what the rate was or if the foreign currency was in cash or offshore bank transfers – the important thing was that the runners got as much foreign currency as possible.

> They needed foreign exchange to fund the vehicles, weapons and other imports for government. So they set up a whole network of street dealers to buy forex. We have two ex-employees of the Reserve Bank who work for us now. They tell us of meeting Reserve Bank officials at the bottom of the building. These officials had trunks full of cash notes, which the runners took to the streets to trade.
>
> – Financial manager at a large trading company

Later, the commercial banks entered the street market for foreign currency as well. The value of the Zimbabwe dollar collapsed as the huge supply of newly printed money hit the streets.

By then, few people – not even the banks – would hold Zimbabwe dollars for any length of time since the currency was depreciating so fast.

> *When one of the banks went bankrupt, we went in to do an audit. The bank had not been keeping any cash on hand. They had taken all of their cash and converted it into 'hard assets', having bought pick-up trucks, bricks and the like. This was being done across the board. Even the banks weren't holding on to cash…though this was crazy given that this is their role: to hold on to other people's money!*
>
> – An official at the Reserve Bank of Zimbabwe

Banks Were Forced to Lend Money

In an attempt to 'support' unskilled new farmers who had taken farmland in the government land grabs, the Reserve Bank forced banks to lend to the farmers and the mines. These loans, called ASPEF loans (Agricultural Sector Productive Enhancement Facility), were mostly given to the politically connected. They would use them to profit by purchasing US dollars on the black market or listed shares, the price of which went through the roof in line with inflation, making the loans repayable with ease.

Taxation Gets Replaced By Money Printing

One of the many bizarre and self-defeating effects of hyperinflation was to wipe out the government's tax income totally. When company tax was due at the end of the tax year, the amount owed to the government had depreciated in value. The time taken for companies to be charged for taxes caused inflation to erode the purchasing power of the amount due, becoming almost valueless. This forced the government to print more money and confiscate more foreign currency to replace the lost tax income.

One CEO I interviewed explained it like this:

> *The benefit of hyperinflation is that our tax was effectively nil. By the time the annual payment had been calculated the amount due was negligible. The government tried many different ways of taxing, including a 'pay-as-you-go' type of arrangement, but it never worked. The government's tax base fell to nothing. They collected nothing from companies or individuals, and nothing on import duties. PAYE (the employee tax) reduced significantly because of the huge amount of unemployment.*

> *As far as imports are concerned, the government was mainly interested in import duties, although the duty system was run on the official exchange rate, which was far below the market rate. The amount that we had to pay on imports became negligible. The government couldn't allow their own departments to charge anything other than the official rate – doing otherwise would have exposed their system.*

> *The real tax was the 25% effective levy on US dollar balances in the foreign currency accounts, and the inflation tax that government had funded through printing money.*

110

Transaction Control: Chete Forces His Friends to Play the Game

[We] organised a march against the government but the police and army drove around to the front in an armoured car, dropped the doors and had four machine guns at the ready to fire on the crowd. It was an effective tactic…and [we] dispersed very quickly.

*   *   *

We had no strength as individuals comparative to the power of the government.

— Comments by various Zimbabweans

Zimbabwe's government became more coercive and manipulative, forcing people to use Zimbabwe dollars and to keep prices low. Money and prices are an integral part of daily life – there are practically few things in life that are not directly connected to money and prices. As the government tried to control the use of money and the level of prices, so it began to have complete involvement in every area of life. It used the various tools to control the population in this regard.

Liquidity Obfuscation

Since becoming a central banker, I have learned to mumble with great incoherence. If I seem unduly clear to you, you must have misunderstood what I said.

> – **Alan Greenspan**, former chairman of the US Federal Reserve

The authorities had to gain a firm mastery of the words it used in order to direct the way people understood their experiences of hyperinflation. Have you ever listened to bankers or politicians and had no idea what they were saying? Often this is intentional. People can get confused to no end when they encounter fancy jargon.

You probably had the same experience with the title of this section. *Liquidity obfuscation* is a complex way of saying, *making money printing vague and difficult to understand.* When you read it, you probably glazed over it and allowed your mind to block it out. It's a typical response for most people – instead of questioning jargon, you'd rather disengage and accept the intellectual authority of the person speaking.

This principle of linguistic relativity is popularly known as the Sapir-Whorf hypothesis. The hypothesis suggests that language controls thought and that specific use of language can be used to influence thought patterns and control behaviour. It further views that a people-group's worldview and cultural understanding are deeply shaped by their language. 'Possession of a common language is still and will continue to be a smoother of the way to a mutual understanding,' Sapir said. Those who define that common language define the understanding.

Governing authorities around the world use word gymnastics to keep people fooled about what they are doing. In his bestselling book, *1984*, George

Orwell called it *doublethink*. Others call it *doublespeak*. The purpose is to distort the meaning of words deliberately and to disguise the nature of the truth. It was, as Orwell later said, '*to make lies sound truthful and murder respectable, and to give an appearance of solidity to pure wind*'.

The Reserve Bank of Zimbabwe described its money printing plans using clever phrases and terminology. When it dropped zeros from the currency, it called it the Zero *to Hero* campaign, suggesting that people were heroes for helping restore the currency to normal values. When it increased its currency denominations to Z$50 billion notes, it named them *special agro-cheques*, because the agricultural industry needed larger denominations. It also used the name *bearer cheques*. There was no real distinction between special agro-cheques, bearer cheques, and previous types of currency, except now the Reserve Bank could talk freely about printing money while still sounding very official and sensible: '*Increasing the number of bearer cheques in the economy*' sounds a lot less alarming than '*printing boat loads of money*'.

In extending the language of transaction control, when shops increased prices, the government branded the store owners as *profiteers*, and those companies that withheld sales because official prices were too low were labelled *hoarders*.

If a government can define words, it can control how concepts are understood. And, if it is worried that people will reject those concepts, it can phrase them in such complex ways that opponents will simply be too befuddled to dispute them.

All central banks use liquidity obfuscation. The term quantitative easing is a great example, as are the numerous other money printing schemes the Federal Reserve announced in 2008: the *Commercial Paper Funding Facility*, the *Term Asset Backed Securities Loan Facility*, the *Primary Dealer Credit Facility* and the *Term Securities Lending Facility*. They all sound so very complex and controlled, and yet their meaning, which even many experts fail to understand fully, is *sending lots of newly printed money to banks and the government so they can stay in business!*

Price Control

Obscure language is one thing, but when Zimbabwe's government began to control prices, it intensified the economic suffering of ordinary people. This was a radical move. Since prices and transactions are a part of everyday life, it meant that the government got involved at every level of society. There are many stories of the Pricing Control Commission going into stores to confiscate goods off the shelves for breach of pricing regulations, allowing government officials to steal goods in the process.

Mines and farms that produced key commodities were named *special industries,* and the government instituted centralised buying. All resources and farm produce had to be sold to the government directly at the official rate. The government would sell it directly to the global market and take any mark-up for itself – which, of course, just fed the den of corruption of the politically connected. This, too, was unsustainable. Farmers had rapidly rising input costs and the official sales prices didn't cover these costs.

A subtle yet powerful means of price control is to fiddle with official inflation statistics. In times of extreme money printing, governments

become craftier and more brazen in distorting official data to keep people from turning to alternatives.[35] This is exactly what happened in Zimbabwe. If the government can make people believe inflation is lower than it really is, it can suppress expectations of inflation and so retard the rise in some prices. Under-reporting actual inflation also allows government to get away with large divergence between official prices it pays for things and the real market prices.

Forcing People to Use Banks

Governments typically control transactions by monitoring and controlling the banking system. It is nearly impossible for anyone to control what people do with cash, but electronic bank transactions are easily monitored, recorded and controlled.

The government therefore made it illegal to trade with big physical cash amounts or to hold large amounts of cash, trying to force people to deposit it with the banks. Yet those who had money in the banks still lined up to withdraw cash at ATMs to get their money out. In response, the Reserve Bank instituted strict withdrawal limits, which were a fraction of the amount of money people typically had in their accounts. Eventually, the amount of money people were allowed to withdraw per day wouldn't even pay for a minibus taxi ride back home.

Although draconian, these measures were practically impossible to implement, and Zimbabwe fast became a physical cash society. A social entrepreneur said this of how he got around the withdrawal limits:

> To get cash, we rented other people's bank cards, transferring funds into their bank accounts electronically and then using the card to withdraw money, leaving a small cut for them in their account. Some people used up to 20 bank cards at the same time to withdraw enough cash to go about their daily affairs. It took a lot of effort but was the only way that we could get cash in hand.

Forcing Institutions to Hold Cash and Bonds

The government needed continued funding and turned to companies that held large investments on behalf of other people – in particular, pension funds, asset managers and insurance companies. It borrowed heavily from these companies by forcing them to buy government bonds. As inflation eroded the value of the bonds, these investment companies began to make significant losses, passing on these losses to their clients. A whole generation of people lost their pensions and life savings as their investments were locked in a system of extensive government control.

Policing, Military and Surveillance Agencies

Hard power is a keystone of government control. In an economic crisis, you can be sure that the army and police will be first in line to be looked after, even to the detriment of other important government services. Robert Mugabe kept a firm grip on the military and police from his early days in power. As inflation rates soared, the police and army presence in Zimbabwe had to increase. They were paid comparatively well and were given special privileges, such as being able to ride commuter taxis for free. On numerous occasions, political protests against rising prices were brutally suppressed.

The regime needed to monitor people's behaviour and movements, so it set up numerous spying agencies. The first was the Central Intelligence Organisation, which sought out any political dissent. It worked closely with the Reserve Bank, which had divisions to monitor and control currency transactions. The Pricing Control Commission was established to monitored prices, to approve price increases, and to set prices generally. The rather absurdly named National Economic Conduct Inspectorate provided further surveillance of both local and international transactions.

These surveillance agencies targeted, among others, business leaders with threats of imprisonment. They relied more on bully tactics than advanced detective and monitoring techniques. Most in government had their salaries inflating away faster than they could receive increases. With the extreme financial pressure they were under, government officials usually did what they could to catch people just so they could extract a bribe.

> *An elderly lady who worked for us part-time went to buy books for the orphans we helped. She purchased a stack of books and paid the bookseller in US dollars. Just then an undercover government agent pounced. We were forced to pay a bribe. I hate bribes, but when the choice is watching an elderly lady go to jail or paying a bribe, you pay the bribe.*
>
> – Head of a non-profit organisation

At one stage, hundreds of headmasters and headmistresses were arrested for fee increases at their schools.

> *They arrested many school principals as part of a blitz against increases. I kept a roll of toilet paper on the desk and an appropriate coat behind the door in expectation of the moment that I would be arrested. Since we could only wear two items of clothing in jail, the coat had to be a big one! All the school principals in our area did the same.*
>
> – Headmistress

Courts, Judges and Prisons

The justice system in Zimbabwe became corrupted as the government replaced experienced judges with political cronies. Courts soon developed into arms of state control, and as hyperinflation ravaged the country, the penal system of fines and prison management completely broke down. By the time the fines were argued in court and prosecuted, their value had become worthless from inflation. The myriad of invasive laws made everyone a criminal, so the prisons soon became overcrowded and were hopelessly underfunded. Prison guards were underpaid, and corruption flourished as justice became a matter of bribery and favours.

One CEO of a large company was caught receiving a salary in an offshore bank account:

> *We were a listed company at the time. A number of politically connected individuals used their access to newly printed money to buy out the company in one go. We were cruising along with a board that was deeply connected to our business and which had secretly approved offshore salaries for its executives. In one day the entire board was*

replaced with government officials. It put us in a tough position because we knew they suspected us. We couldn't trust the very board that we reported to. We began to delete any information on our computers that made reference to illegal activities – which in itself was illegal.

Within a month, the NECI came to audit us. They were dark-suited shady characters who wore sunglasses – how we imagined the CIA or the FBI in America. When they arrived at our offices, they took the executives into our boardroom and one by one escorted each of us to our offices. They went through every email and every document in all of our files and then proceeded to search the toilets and other rooms in the building. They were looking for any evidence showing that we had paid salaries in foreign currency. The senior leaders took me aside and said, 'Right, we know everything you have done. If you don't own up to it we will put you and your wife in jail.' It was a hair-raising time!

The agency was there for several weeks, going through our processes with a fine-tooth comb. Eventually they found one email authorising the offshore transfers.

They found out earlier in the week, but only arrested us on the Friday – bail applications were heard during weekdays so we had to spend the weekend in jail. This was standard for the spy agencies. It was a way of hassling people without either fining them or putting them in prisons long term after expensive legal proceedings.

That day, they arrested five of our executives. My wife and friends took oranges and chickens for the guards at the cells to ensure that we were treated okay.

As part of the bail terms, I had to report to the court every Monday and Friday. The NECI then indefinitely delayed court proceedings. It was the biggest headache and made my life a misery for two years. Eventually when the court date did come, they produced proof of the offshore account and I was told that if I paid all my foreign funds to the government, the charges would be dropped. I gratefully gave them everything I had.

Media and Centres of Influence

Control the media and you can control the message. Zimbabwe's government knew this all too well. It closed down media companies that weren't sympathetic to its interests – which were most of them! Only two newspapers remained, *The Herald* and *The Standard* – both were state-controlled. All foreign journalists were banned from the country, and several were arrested.

Many churches were infiltrated by spy agencies and numerous church leaders were arrested for speaking out against the government. In the rural areas, tribal leaders were kept under keen surveillance. Rural towns and villages experienced violent protests in reaction to the government's overbearing control. But the government held firm, doing everything in its power to control the flow of information, how it was heard and how it was interpreted.

Politics of Printed Money in a Nugget

How you respond to government control is a defining feature of surviving hyperinflation. In almost every country the world over, central banks print

paper money and lend it to commercial banks. Commercial banks then 'print' electronic bank credit money and lend to people like you and me. They also lend this to the government. The government uses the central bank and the commercial banks to create more money for itself to fund its expenses, manipulate markets and benefit special interest groups. With an unlimited chequebook, Zimbabwe's government could spend as it pleased. However, tax income fell significantly, eroded by inflation, and the authorities had to rely more and more on newly printed money and confiscation (theft) of foreign currency to fund its expenses.

As inflation increased and ordinary Zimbabweans lost confidence in Zimbabwe dollars, the government resorted to extensive control measures; they managed prices, fiddled with inflation rates, and used obscure language that made it difficult to understand definitively what was going on or to criticise effectively. To control the message further, a host of new laws needed to be passed to keep control of the public, particularly to control bank transactions and everyday trade. An important component was an enlarged police and military presence to implement these laws; the justice and penal systems developed into tools of state coercion. Almost everyone became a criminal as petty laws proliferated and regulations became ways in which the state could extract bribes and fines to try fill up its barren coffers. Finally, the media and the local centres of influence were infiltrated and forced to toe the government's line.

Think About It

1. To what degree is your government increasing its control over the population?

2. Does it use *word gymnastics* in public comments?

3. If the government made ordinary behaviour a crime, would you disobey the laws?

PART II

Hyperinflation: The Personal Experience

"Every day, before I came home, I would pop into the shops to see what I could buy. The shelves would typically be empty..."

– Zimbabwean housewife

In the first part of this book, we examined why and how hyperinflation happens and what it looks like economically. In discussing the economic principles of hyperinflation, it can be easy to forget how this kind of crisis affects society in deeply practical and personal ways. Zimbabwe gives us fascinating and sometimes jarring insights into the daily challenges that ordinary people from all walks of life can face during the chaos of hyperinflation. The stories in this section highlight how ordinary people responded to the pressures of rapidly rising prices.

Take a moment to consider how prices affect your daily life. There are thousands of prices you interact with on a daily basis. Most of us expect these prices to stay more or less the same from one day to the next – it is something we take for granted. What would you do if prices started to rise uncontrollably? When prices soar, it places people under severe and sustained pressure that is probably unlike anything you have ever experienced. This section of the book gives crucial insight into some of those pressures, with real life examples of how people have responded to extraordinary and distressing circumstances.

Chapter 7

The Economics of Hunger

There was no food anywhere. You couldn't find basic supplies in any store, not even milk…and yet there was always enough beer. I don't recall us ever not having beer.

– Zimbabwean expat in South Africa

It was the end of a lavish family Sunday lunch, the kind that makes your eyelids heavy and draws you towards a long afternoon nap. We'd all finished our meals and were waiting for Nonna Marisa, our Italian grandmother, to be done. Her withered wrinkles told of a long life and great wisdom. Concentrating, she reached slowly for the butter dish and spread large lumps of it on her last remaining chunk of bread.

'Have another piece of bread with your butter, Nonna,' my brother joked.

She smiled a knowing smile and finished it off, bread slice and lump of butter.

She paused to think before stretching out a knobbled finger. 'You young people have never known what hunger is. You have never felt the pain of it. If you had, you would know how wonderful it is to have butter.'

Nonna grew up in the southern part of Italy in well-off circumstances. Her family were wealthy Neapolitans who owned numerous properties in the south of the country. She grew up without a care and had everything she needed.

But in the dark days of World War II, the entire community experienced food shortages unlike anything they had ever known. When the American army arrived, the locals begged them for food. For a long time, Nonna considered butter and olive oil as precious luxuries. She never forgot her experience, nor did she lose her sense of gratitude for food.

Hyperinflation Forced Stores to Close Down

The food shortages Nonna experienced were a result of war, but in Zimbabwe they were the result of the ravages of hyperinflation. As is normal in modern economies, most relied on stores for the provision of daily necessities such as food, and as the stores emptied, food supply became a critical and desperate problem. It wasn't just grocery stores that emptied; it was *all* stores. People could no longer get ordinary retail goods from the shops. If you wanted something, you had to find alternative ways to get it.

Hyperinflation pushed retailers to bankruptcy. As store owners raised prices to stay in business, the government fought back with price controls in warlike fashion. The Price Control Commission was set up to regulate prices. Hundreds of store owners were arrested for trying to stay in business, being accused of 'profiteering'. Price control agents confiscated shops' entire stock as penalty for raising prices. It became a formalised means of looting. Agents made off with flat-screen TVs, foods of all kinds and other goods.

Price controls caused shop owners to stop supplying goods to the public. In their zeal to control prices, the government ended up making the shortages far worse, which only served to force the market price of goods higher.

Further compounding the folly, the government made it illegal to *cease* supplying. It tried to force the retailers to continue providing goods, but this only achieved one thing: worse shortages and closure of entire industries. Large retailers had to stay open and keep their staff, even though the shops were practically bare. They always seemed to find at least one item to keep on the shelves – a loose toilet roll or a bottle of jam placed on the odd shelf in otherwise naked aisles.

> *Understandably, we went bankrupt. Who can continue profitably in such circumstances? When we were confronted by Pricing Control, we blamed our lack of supply on the manufacturers who had increased their prices. The PC agents then went, with large mobs of rioting youth, to the various factories to force them to reduce prices.*
>
> *The manufacturers couldn't decrease their prices either without going out of business – they had input prices set by world markets. Quickly, the whole supply chain shut down. By the middle of 2006, there weren't any stores that had any goods in them. It was an absolute tragedy.*

– CEO of a retail company

Hyperinflation Caused Mass Hunger

Desperation set in. Suddenly, towns, cities and rural areas that had come to rely heavily on sophisticated 'just-in-time' supply systems were highly exposed. The smaller towns in the rural areas were particularly vulnerable.

Everyone living in these places had lived their lives on the assumptions that goods would be delivered to stores that were close to them. When this stopped, the entire makeup of these urban areas changed. As hyperinflation destroyed the economy, it left families frantically searching for their next meal.

> When we went into the supermarkets, all the people who worked there were just standing around. The shelves were empty and there was no food to be found anywhere. It was bloody scary.

One executive I interviewed told us his heart-rending difficulties in how it affected his factory workers:

> Our staff were all very thin and it became a great problem for our business. We had instances of staff fainting from hunger. Eventually we paid them out in food boxes when we had access to them.

Another interviewee said:

> With the massive shutdown of industry, millions were left without jobs and without access to food. I don't know how they survived.

Each time a grain truck passed through rural areas, a steady queue of mothers carrying children on their backs sprang up seemingly from nowhere. They were waiting to pick up the few kernels of grain that fell onto the side of the road. Hunger was such a major problem in these parts that desperate people even ate bark from trees.

If the Shops Can't Get Us Food, the Government Must!

Food became a hot political issue. The ruling political party began to supply grain and food to rural communities, which became a useful way of

ensuring political support, as well as punishing lack of support. In addition to oppressive policing and army control, food supply was a useful way to maintain the party's hold on power.

The opposition party cottoned on to this strategy and also began supplying food to communities. In response, the government made it illegal for anyone to transport large quantities of food without a government licence. If someone wanted to get food aid into a particular area they would have to pay bribes to police along the highway, just to help starving communities. Not only were shops emptying, but individuals couldn't even supply food to their own families in the smaller towns without government approval. This politicisation of food set the scene for major political violence in the rural areas, particularly as food became scarcer and the people more desperate.

As food shortages worsened, and as government food distribution became more corrupt, starvation in the rural areas grew to be endemic. The Zimbabwean government covered up and suppressed information about this tragic episode, so the statistics are unavailable – but those Zimbabweans we interviewed generally estimated that *hundreds of thousands* of people ended up starving to death, particularly outside the main cities.

Possibly the most gut-wrenching quote on the desperation of hyperinflation comes from Adam Fergusson's gripping account of Germany's hyperinflation in his book, *When Money Dies*.

In war, boots; in flight, a place in a boat or a seat on a lorry may be the most vital thing in the world, more desirable than untold millions. In hyperinflation, a kilo of potatoes was worth, to some, more than the family silver; a side of pork more than the grand piano. A prostitute in the family was better than an infant corpse; theft was preferable to starvation; warmth was finer than honour, clothing more essential than democracy, food more needed than freedom.

If Not From Shops or Government, Where Else Do We Get Food?

The government was not involved in supplying food to city and suburban areas, and as a result, people turned to the only way they could live in these circumstances: community support. Those who survived developed sophisticated barter systems of trade. Communities drew closer. Everyone had to develop relational connections for the supply of some form of food – if you didn't plug into relational networks, your chances of surviving were slim. Quickly, formal distribution networks morphed into crude but effective relational supply chains.

Most people who had lived all their lives relying on their local supermarkets and cafés to supply them with their daily food and lifestyle needs suddenly had to make alternative plans or go without. Apart from the politically connected few who had access to government stores of food, the shortages were universal. All people in Zimbabwe had this problem, from the wealthiest to the poorest of the poor.

Meat Matters

My husband and I did not eat meat for a full year. It was scarce up to that point, but by 2008 we just couldn't get it anywhere – we were both high-level professionals in our various industries and yet it was too expensive for us.

– Woman based in Harare

As the wave of farmland invasions swept across Zimbabwe, farmers were left with no choice but to slaughter and sell entire herds before their land was taken. Prices for meat had been rising in shops, but suddenly a day came when meat prices dropped as the glut hit the market. As the price fell, it forced other uncertain farmers to slaughter their cattle as well for fear that prices might keep falling. Suddenly, Zimbabweans everywhere could buy as much meat as they wanted at affordable prices. The joy was short-lived though. The glut was followed by chronic shortages after the commercial livestock throughout the country were consumed. Meat all but disappeared, and meat prices rocketed. People could only get it through their barter networks.

Meat was one of the hardest commodities to trade. Live cows couldn't be transported because of government restrictions, but once a cow had been slaughtered, the meat would perish quickly. Power cuts caused freezers full of frozen goods to defrost within a day without electricity. Fresh meat eventually could only be sourced very selectively on the black market.

One night, my brother called me on my cell phone. 'I've found some meat,' he whispered barely audibly. 'Meet me at the back of the train station in half an hour.' We shot through straight away and met him in the dark of night. In the boot of his car our shining torches revealed half a bloodied ox on a plastic lining. Right then and there, with an old axe and large cutting knife, we chopped it into pieces. And out of the night came the customers. We sold the entire boot's contents by the end of the evening!

– Father of three based in Harare

Other Food Shortages

It wasn't just meat that was short in supply – even bread was scarce. People had to queue many long hours when it was available. An enterprising woman I interviewed managed to get hold of dough to make bread. In her story we can appreciate the lighter side of hyperinflation.

While there was a control on the price of bread, there was no control on the price of dough. I had heard that there was a supplier of dough in Bulawayo and I was going down there on business. I bought three lots of dough in little packets. Because of the fuel shortage, we couldn't turn on our air conditioner since the car would use more fuel. The drive back from Bulawayo was really hot and I had left the dough on the back seat. In the heat, the dough began to rise.

It grew out of the bowl on the floor and spread out all over the back seats, eventually rising all the way up past the level of the windows – there obviously was quite a bit of yeast in it. As I was driving I saw this hideous growth in the back of my car and panicked! I stretched back to grab at it and it popped and flopped all over the floor. It had spoiled and there was nothing I could do.

Shortages of ground maize became acute. Known locally as *sadza*, it is the staple diet of most Zimbabweans. Deprived of staple foods, people in rural areas turned to hunting. Wild game that used to be abundant in the wilderness areas were all but eradicated.

> *We had both cats and dogs. It was difficult to get ordinary food for us, but next to impossible to find any pet food. We fed the dogs with* sadza *but the cats wouldn't touch it. Instead, my husband would shoot pigeons to feed them!*
>
> — Counsellor and mother of two

Shopping Alternatives

Those who had foreign currency would often 'pop over the border for their monthly shop', which became good business for retailers in neighbouring South Africa and Botswana. It was the last source of quality retail goods that most city dwellers had become so accustomed to.

In Woodmead, Johannesburg, a large retail discount store called Makro saw the opportunity and set up an entire section of its store for Zimbabwean shoppers. It was hugely successful, selling Zimbabweans specially stacked pallets of bulk goods. Back in Zimbabwe, this option became so popular that business deals were often quoted in *Woodmead Makro Pallets*, the equivalent of a standard pallet of goods from the store.

Once goods had been purchased and stacked on a pallet, they needed to be transported. A transport network developed with numerous couriers specialising in moving Makro pallets across the border.

This developed into an online system where Zimbabweans could order directly on the Internet, pay in foreign currency and have delivery made to their houses. However, this option was only available to those who had offshore bank accounts denominated in South African rand.

Bartering

Those who didn't have access to food from abroad had to source locally from others within their community. Most of this was by barter. Each individual had to become a specialist provider of a particular food or good in his or her community.

> Since we had to source food through our relational networks, there was simply no access to luxuries such as soft drinks, chips or other fast food. Sugar was so precious that few people consumed it in unhealthy quantities.

> Apart from the politicians who were all tubby, we had few overweight people about.

> The only food we could get was locally grown vegetables that were absolutely organic and grown in backyards – no one had money for fertilisers or pesticides; and certainly no one could get expensive genetically engineered seeds.

Most people in the developed world don't have the first clue about how to kill, de-feather and gut a chicken, let alone slaughter, skin, gut and quarter a cow. How many people would then have the stomach to eat the animals

134

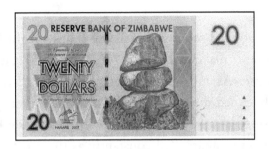

they've just killed? During hyperinflation, these questions become more than just hypothetical!

How Do You Get Clean Without Soap?

You are most probably used to having access to numerous everyday goods that you can buy from the store. It's what adds to your quality of life. If you need something, anything, you just pop into the nearby mall outlet to get it, often paying by card. These simple conveniences disappeared during hyperinflation and for those who had lived their lives based on supermarket supply chains, life became much more difficult.

Toilet paper was extremely difficult to get hold of. Have you ever considered what alternatives you would use for toilet paper? Tissues perhaps. Wet wipes maybe. Newspaper? Handkerchiefs? Store shelves were emptying, so none of these alternatives were readily available either.

What about other sanitation needs? What would you do without soap, toothpaste and other cleaning materials? When they aren't available, what would your alternative be? Some people made their own soap. Some went without. Others got it through connections in their network. Many purchased these items in other countries.

These are examples of the lifestyle pressures ordinary Zimbabweans were under as the goods they'd come to rely on became rare finds in the ordinary course of life. It applied to all goods in the shops – light bulbs, candles, clothing, deodorant, makeup and hair products, TVs, computers and all other merchandise. As inflation ravaged the country, the formal retail sector effectively closed down and people had to get their goods through other means. Most learned to be thrifty with what they had and made do without. Living standards fell constantly as the value of the currency plummeted.

Fuel: The Energy of an Economy

Fuel was one of the more difficult commodities to obtain. The fuel shortages started early in 2000, but as the fires of inflation raged, it became almost impossible to get any. Fuel is a crucial commodity that everyone needs every day in both direct and indirect ways, for transport of people and things. Fuel became the source of electricity for many who were using generators when electricity was cut.

Fuel stations continually had long queues of cars winding from their forecourts. Many people slept in their vehicles while waiting successive days to fill their tanks. When fuel eventually arrived, usually only those at the front of the queue received it. One interviewee had this to say:

> Our friends who worked at the BP and Shell stations would let us know if a truck was coming. The news travelled quickly and queues formed immediately. It took so much time away from our business, so we paid drivers to queue for fuel for us. The idle queues became quite festive – since there was little to do during the time and everyone had to sit and wait, the time turned into great social events that crossed every cultural and ethnic barrier. We met many people during that time.

Other Personal Goods

It's not just a shortage of food or cleaning materials that are a concern in times of hyperinflation. Think of all the personal items you use on a daily basis that bring you creature comforts.

One transparent waitress had this to say:

> Finding tampons was another task, all told. You couldn't readily get them in the shops. The only way I could find any was to get from my network – it's funny to talk about it now. We were all going through the same thing so it wasn't embarrassing; it was just one of those vulnerable things you did. I'd tell the ladies in the most surreptitious way, 'Hey…it's my time.' We all understood and somehow the community would get you what you needed. Eventually, an eco-friendly silicone Mooncup became available from the UK. These reusable devices were an instant hit in Zimbabwe. For those who had children I can't even imagine how difficult it must have been to get baby goodies.

Makeup and hair products were luxuries that most did without. In many ways, people went back to more primitive living.

Economics of Hunger in a Nugget

Lofty economic terms such as hyperinflation and velocity of money had very real implications for the quality of life of everyone on the ground. Stores emptied as the real effects of money printing hit home. Food, sanitation and other products and services people took for granted became extremely difficult to find, and sourcing them often took hours of time and effort. Mass hunger became acute and many thousands of people died of starvation.

In a few very short years, people's needs became so basic. They worked for food, a toilet roll or a bar of soap – simple goods that made a profound difference in everyday comfort levels. In short, the consumption-frenzied economy made normal goods incredibly scarce, and people succumbed to ever more encroaching poverty, living for their day-to-day survival and unsure of where their next meal was going to come from.

Think About It

1. If the shops emptied, how would you get your food and basic necessities?

2. How easy is it for you to produce your own food?

3. Do you have strong enough community relationships to build reliable relational supply networks?

4. Would you be able to kill an animal for food?

Chapter 8

Government Shutdown

All basic government services gradually disappeared...All except the police.

— Bus driver

It had been a 14-hour ride from Johannesburg to Harare, and I was feeling grimy in a way that only a long bus trip can make you feel. It was my latest fact-finding trip to Zimbabwe and I was relieved to see my host, Steve, as he arrived to pick me up.

'Gosh, I can't wait for a hot shower to clean off,' I said.

Perhaps it was the travel weariness, but I didn't notice the awkward silence.

His home was large and spacious, and on arrival, the domestic helper, Aunty, ushered me through to my room. After a brief conversation with Steve, she indicated that I could have a bath. Not being the bathing type, I politely declined and asked for a shower instead. Only when I got to the bathroom did I understand. There in the unused shower was a handheld tub filled with lukewarm water and next to it, a neatly folded washcloth. The water came from numerous containers around Steve's house that Aunty had stove-heated using a generator. My 'bath' consisted of me soaping and rinsing myself from the tub using a wet cloth. As I hunkered there, wiping myself down, hyperinflation became real in a way I hadn't understood before.

That wasn't the end of it either. They had no running water to flush the toilets. I couldn't even have a decent shave. I've spent most of my life in suburban Johannesburg, where a daily shower and multiple bathroom visits are an absolute minimum for any form of sanity. Like stable prices, when these things you take for granted disappear, quality of life plummets instantly.

*   *   *

During hyperinflation, government departments and municipal services are the least likely to survive. Almost all of Zimbabwe's municipal services collapsed. No one could depend on even the most basic of comforts, such as access to clean running water.

If well-organised businesses were folding, you can imagine how quickly inefficient municipal services collapsed. Costs soared, yet municipal pricing and billing structures were slow, bureaucratic, and couldn't keep pace with inflation. Inputs and components that had to be imported were priced in foreign currencies, but municipalities had to charge for services in Zimbabwe dollars. By the time these municipalities received payments for their already under-priced services, the payments were worth much less in real terms. This crippled municipal cashflow and not even government bailouts could prevent deterioration in the quality of their services.

The painstaking bureaucracy of wage setting and trade union negotiations meant municipalities couldn't raise salaries fast enough, and since they

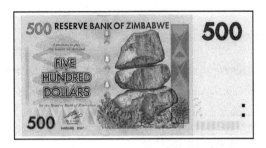

were forbidden to pay their staff in foreign currency, the purchasing power of municipal wages plunged. Most skilled staff emigrated in droves. People in municipal salaried positions often had to subsidise their salaries either by trading on the side or through corrupt means.

David Matthee, a small business owner in Harare, highlighted the dilemma well:

> In my business, if I didn't find alternative currencies to trade in I would have gone bankrupt. It was all highly illegal and if I got caught, the penalty would have been severe. But I had to do so to feed my family. You can imagine though that no one working in a bureaucratic position in government would be willing to take the risk. No government worker would risk a jail sentence for the sake of his department.

> The government forced civil services to accept cheque payments and bank transfers. We readily used cheques to pay our municipal expenses because by the time they cleared, the amounts paid from our bank accounts were a fraction of the initial purchasing power value.

In the excesses of hyperinflation, municipalities became unviable. The government tried to keep facilities going – they even made newly printed money directly available to state entities – but they could not keep up, and inevitably, most municipal departments went bankrupt.

Water & Sewerage

I went for over eight months without any municipal water and got so very depressed. It was the lack of water that got me down. You can live without electricity but you can't live without water.

– Widowed mother

What would you do if you couldn't get running water? Throughout Zimbabwe, water treatment facilities fell into disrepair. Water supply was intermittent at best, and the standard of purification was dreadful. Water treatment chemicals were expensive and, like equipment and spare parts, had to be imported. Water engineers resigned, leaving less-skilled staff to apply purifying chemicals. The result was untrustworthy water quality. It is rumoured that at one stage, the staff at the water department, who had almost no skills or training, got the chemicals confused and almost put arsenic in the water.

Dams and piping networks fell to pieces. Frequent water cuts meant air regularly got into the piping system, causing parts of it to rust and break. Water in underground pipes seeped away silently, and burst pipes gushed their wasted contents down the streets.

David Matthee continued:

They couldn't charge us anywhere near what was appropriate. Their billing systems always ran a month or two behind and by the time we paid the bill, it was small relative to price increases. Electricity and water payments were such miniscule amounts, it's a wonder that the services continued for as long as they did. I have no idea how those departments lasted so long.

Sewerage treatment plants had the same problems. In high-density areas, sewage flowed openly in the streets and ran into rivers. In some places, sewerage pipes leaked into the water pipes, giving rise to regular Cholera outbreaks.

Zimbabweans' responses to water shortages were very resourceful. Many houses had access to boreholes – sophisticated wells tapped into underground lakes. The water table in Zimbabwe has historically been quite high, so this was an easy solution for many people. An active black market developed for water. People who had borehole water tapped it into large tanks and sold it to those who didn't have their own water sources.

Some were extremely successful in finding solutions to problems concerning domestic water supply. A number of smart, inventive people developed their houses to be as free from municipal supply dependence as possible, using innovative home-made engineering solutions, creating mini-dams filled by various drainage systems. Many bought large water tanks, which they would fill with borehole water, and municipal water when it was flowing. Those who had swimming pools were at an advantage since these were the largest water tanks of the lot.

But even with elaborate systems, people had to be highly conscious of their water usage. Some used leftover bathwater for the toilets. Self-rationing was non-negotiable.

Electricity: The Power Behind All We Do

What did Zimbabweans have before candles? We had electricity!

– Zimbabwean joke

Next on the list of critical shortages was electricity. The Zimbabwe Electricity Supply Authority (ZESA), the state-owned electricity supplier, suffered all the same problems as other municipal and state-run services.

Not only did ZESA find it difficult to source inputs and to fund escalating costs, but it was also burdened with massive theft problems. Copper cables and transformers that provided electricity to entire districts were stolen on a regular basis. Copper was something that could readily be exchanged for goods or cash in the milieu of economic devastation, and so widespread cable theft became a significant problem for ZESA – it was too easy an option for desperate people.

Turbines at the power stations needed ongoing maintenance, and without it they finally broke down. Zimbabwe could, in times past, generate so much electricity that it supplied neighbouring countries, but eventually most of the country's electricity needs had to be imported from South Africa.

> *To compensate, we got the 'Rolls-Royce' of generators. It made such a noise and the smell was awful. We never got used to that. Every night when we turned it off, a burden lifted from our shoulders as the night air returned to silence.*

*   *   *

We'd often use the camping equipment – candles, gas lamps and rechargeable LED lights that lasted for 25 hours.

* * *

I installed a large battery inverter system. As soon as the power cut off, it would kick in. The charge was not enough for everything, just for the computers and what we really needed.

Fridges, stoves and other heavy electrical consumption equipment had to be turned off. You can imagine how difficult it was to keep food fresh. We had a rule that no one could open the freezer during the blackout times.

* * *

The blackouts forced us to become less reliant on computers, so much of our business was done with pen or pencil.

>   – Various Zimbabweans on their responses to the
>   electricity shortages

Most people didn't have the money to purchase a generator, and if they did buy one, few could find the fuel to run it. So to stay warm in winter, many burned wood in fireplaces or drums, and cooked over an open flame. Countless free-standing trees in public spaces were cut down to be used as fuel.

How would you survive if you didn't have any electricity? You use dozens of household items that require electrical inputs. If those couldn't be used any more, what would you do? How would your quality of life be affected if you couldn't use, for instance, washing machines, tumble dryers, dishwashers, fridges, microwaves and stoves, hairdryers, geysers, computers or rechargeable cell phones? In Zimbabwe, these modern necessities became obsolete without access to electricity.

Other Municipal Services

The municipalities stopped providing all forms of infrastructure maintenance and refuse removal. The whole structure and support network for dams, roads and schools fell apart. Street and traffic lights stopped working, so many intersections became four-way stops. Roads were lined with litter. Prison systems collapsed and thousands of prisoners died as penitentiaries couldn't provide basic food and water to inmates.

Government hospitals ground to a halt. Deteriorating health conditions affected poor people the most. They could no longer get proper care. Local medical aid companies went bankrupt, putting affordable health care out of reach for most Zimbabweans. It became difficult to get even the most basic of medicines, such as antibiotics, anti-inflammatories and asthma pumps. People couldn't go across the border and purchase medicine, like they could for other goods. Neighbouring countries typically restricted the purchase of drugs without a local doctor's prescription. All hospitals stopped providing major treatments, including cancer care. Power would often go off in the middle of operations, which made surgery risky. With water cuts, hospitals couldn't clean properly, and disposal of medical waste was haphazard. The once pristine, world-class hospitals became derelict and hazardous, and doctors and specialists flooded out of the country.

Schooling also fell apart.

> *I attended school at Plumtree High School, which was once 'the Eton of Zimbabwe'. When I returned recently, they had no beds in the boarding school. The scholars slept on mats. They had no tables and no equipment. Their textbooks were all photocopied – if the photocopiers could be repaired. The schools all went to rack and ruin.*
>
> – Politician who served in public education

The two government services that were sustained were the police and the military. The government knew well enough that these were the key to its continued power and so did what it could to keep these two departments funded and operational, even at the cost of the other services.

Government Shutdown in a Nugget

In Zimbabwe, municipalities couldn't continue supplying critical services as they went bankrupt. The cost of inputs increased faster than customer tariffs. Critical staff departed in droves. Systems broke down and vital equipment fell into disrepair. Whatever municipal services remained in operation were mostly wasted as distribution networks broke down.

In particular, water services were heavily disrupted, as were electricity and telecommunications. Hospitals, prisons, public schools and general infrastructure became derelict. The police and military were the only government services that survived this difficult period, but these quickly ceased to be public services and came to serve the political ends of the ruling elites.

Think About It

1. To what extent do you rely on government services for your quality of life? If these services were removed, would you be able to survive?

2. How reliant are you on municipal electricity supply, and what you would do without it?

3. Do you have alternative options for water supply?

Chapter 9

Strength in Community

It was the best of times, it was the worst of times, it was the age of wisdom, it was the age of foolishness, it was the epoch of belief, it was the epoch of incredulity, it was the season of Light, it was the season of Darkness, it was the spring of hope, it was the winter of despair, we had everything before us, we had nothing before us ...

– **Charles Dickens**, A Tale of Two Cities

Andrew, our milk supplier, owned a few cows, which he milked daily by hand. An accountant by trade, he had lost his job soon after the crash. When his wife had fallen ill, he bought the cows to help with expenses.

Our milk rendezvous point was always at the back of the golf club late on Saturday afternoons in the shadows of the parking lot. Buying milk this way was highly illegal so we never arrived in groups bigger than three or four.

We'd always see him arriving from afar in an old Toyota, hitched with a rickety trailer carrying three big black dustbins – treasure hidden from the prying eyes of the police. The bins were called 'chigubs' – a local name derived from the scooping sound made when a jug passed through the milk. Cheegoooop!

The tubs opened to reveal a fortune – thick fresh milk full of cream, mixed in with a few tiny floating blades of grass in a rich lather. Some days we would arrive late, only to get the very last of the tub; like diluted tea, it was thin and watery pale blue. The chigubs were washed with bleach so the milk always had a tinge of ammonia to the taste, particularly the milk from the bottom of the barrel. We tried not to notice; it was always just so lovely to have milk.

In return, our gift would be a jerrycan of fuel, chopped wood or anything else we had of value at the time. It was a total barter arrangement. We never paid with money – except if we had foreign exchange, which was rare.

— **Susan Barber**

We were so desperate and our needs so basic, and yet the sense of community was a well supplied by deep waters. Everyone was in the same boat and each of us had an understanding of our responsibility to help one another. It was the grapevine that saved us…

— **Susan Barber 's** daughter-in-law

As we described earlier in this book, there was only one way to survive hyperinflation in Zimbabwe, and that was in *community*. As formal supply chains broke down, an intricate network of community supply evolved throughout the country. Instead of purchasing goods in shops, you had to rely on relationships with people who had access to the food and personal services you needed. In this way, the community developed a bartering network that was practically impossible for the government to control or regulate.

Likewise, as government market manipulation and control increased, so people within the community had to depend on one another for protection and support. The sense of togetherness grew in the trial. Business leaders did what they could to pay their staff salary increases as fast as possible. Customers paid in kind.

Most of the queues took a number of hours to get through – and sometimes days, in the case of the fuel queues, which sprang up everywhere as fuel became increasingly scarce. The only thing to do in these queues was to sit...wait...and socialise! The queues became connection points of great parties with people from all walks of life and diverse backgrounds bonding in a common problem. In the fuel queues, it wasn't uncommon for people to have an impromptu braai (a southern African term for a barbeque) out of the trunk of a car on the roadside, inviting others to join. The queues were festive occasions with great camaraderie.

As businesses closed early, it gave more people time to exercise. Fuel shortages meant people weren't using their cars as much, so they walked a lot more. If anyone had fuel, they gave lifts generously. Many of those we interviewed described how deeply bonding this process was and still speak of it with fondness and nostalgia. In the midst of the darkness, there was tremendous positivity among the people. It was the bright moon in the night of economic collapse.

The daily, personal pressure that everyone was under brought them together in a way they'd never experienced before. While the government tried hard to emphasise various tribal/ racial differences throughout the period, the extreme pressures of day-to-day living drove people closer.

Crime, Theft and the Breakdown of Civil Order

During every great inflation there is a striking decline in both public and private morality.

> – **Henry Hazlitt**, The Inflation Crisis and How To Resolve It

In my research, one of my main points of interest revolved around the criminal response to hyperinflation. I figured that there must have been a breakdown in civil-social order, since there was such widespread lack of basic necessities and failure of the formal supply sector. Surely, I reasoned, if people couldn't get basics such as food and water, they would resort to wholesale theft and violence.

I was amazed at what I found in Zimbabwe. In the midst of economic turmoil, there was relative social peace. The only real violent crime in the country was politically driven.

Diana Blatter, an expert in sociology in Zimbabwe, highlighted this in my interview with her:

> We studied social aspects of development and aid, and one of the questions we asked was, 'Why do some countries descend into chaos, like Somalia or Afghanistan, and why do others not – like Zimbabwe?' Hyperinflation had the most painful effect on society, and yet Zimbabweans still stuck together, waited patiently in queues, and had a respect for law and order throughout the time.

Our conclusions on the matter were that the more fragmented the people in terms of tribes and cultures, the more fragmented they become under extreme pressure like hyperinflation. In Zimbabwe, despite the tribal differences, there are strong associations with being Zimbabwean that transcend tribal allegiances. In other nations, tribal, economic and social allegiances rank higher than a sense of communalism.

Blatter further found that the deep value system shared across the cultures preserved the rule of law. Most Zimbabweans held Christian convictions that guided them to respect the authority of the law, shunning personal aggression and respecting private property, basic social order and contracts. Business was done relationally rather than at arm's length. 'There was a gentleness to Zimbabweans,' Blatter noted, 'that held them together rather than split them apart.'

Most people obeyed the government and the police until the laws became extremely petty. The incidence of muggings at ATMs was very low. Even at the height of the food crises in 1997 and 2003, when food 'riots' broke out, the marches never turned violent, and rarely did participants resort to aggression.

In most cases, people respected one another and understood that those who got to the front of the queues first were entitled to receive first. The only substantial shop looting that took place was done by the price control officers, who would confiscate store contents because of price law 'contraventions'.

Zimbabweans are not a violent people, but another reason for the lack of violence was the effectiveness of the police and the army in putting down violent activity. The government ensured that these divisions were well looked after – given fuel and maize meal rations, along with extra status in society. The riot police, or 'Rovai' as they are known – meaning *beat up* or *hit* in Shona – would brutally maintain crowd control. Violent crime and uprisings were constrained by the threat of severe penalties.

The Paradox of the Culture and the Deterioration of Values

Hyperinflation made everyone a criminal because you had to break the law to survive. We are a nation of law-breakers, forced on us by hyperinflation.

       – CEO of a manufacturing company

Zimbabwean society was a paradox. There was tremendous violence and thievery perpetrated in the name of political power, and yet there was respect and relative peace between individuals and communities of different cultures.

The government, in an attempt to maintain control, stirred violence in the rural areas and townships. Opposition party members were brutally oppressed, while those supporting the ruling party were given special favour. There was violent land occupation in the name of land reform and access to food became a political tool. Increased government surveillance and control resulted in great acts of terror.

Yet, in vast contrast, people felt safe to walk home at night without fear of assault.

Instead of the government fostering order through justice, it used the justice system as a tool to oppress and restrict. Ordinary citizens became accustomed to breaking the myriad of new laws that were issued in an attempt to control the population. Slowly, the formal justice system broke down. Respect for authority deteriorated, and the values held dear within the culture slowly began to erode.

Despite the peaceful culture, hyperinflation wore away at people's ethical resolve over time. As millions were impoverished and government control increased, the only way to survive was through bribery, corruption and illegal activities. To continue about their everyday, peaceful lives, Zimbabweans had to break these laws. The paying and taking of bribes became an accepted norm.

Instead of obedience to the law, people had to use their own personal values and sensibilities in relationships as a guideline for what was wrong or right. Paying someone in US dollars, for example, wasn't considered to be wrong by most people even though it was illegal, while stealing bread was considered wrong.

Yet, slowly values deteriorated with the heightening levels of desperation, and petty theft became frequent. Whatever could be stolen in public spaces disappeared. Anything that was made of wood was used for fire. Any movable metal was taken and sold as scrap. At one stage, all the road signs disappeared, many to be used as rudimentary funnels as barter in fuel increased.

Petty theft grew to be a big problem. There are stories of entire automatic gates being stolen (but very rarely would the thieves then go on to break into the house). Businesses struggled with inventory theft because staff just didn't earn enough money to make ends meet. Truck drivers would siphon off fuel from truck tanks. Farmers' crops and livestock were often stolen – particularly the livestock, which would typically disappear during the night.

In summary, theft revolved around stock shrinkage and theft of public property. Violent and aggressive disrespect for private property, muggings and house break-ins only started becoming a problem once hyperinflation had completely destroyed the economy and social values had deteriorated considerably.

The Exodus

As the conditions for living in Zimbabwe deteriorated, countless Zimbabweans solved their economic problems by migrating. Neighbouring countries, as well as countries on the other side of the world, received millions of fleeing Zimbabweans, not into refugee camps, but by absorbing them into society. Approximately three million Zimbabweans moved to South Africa and many others went to the UK, Canada, Australia, New Zealand, Botswana and Zambia. They are currently known as the Zimbabwe diaspora.

While it is very difficult to get accurate statistics on the diaspora indications are that one-quarter to one-third of Zimbabweans left the country, with over four million moving abroad.

The social effects of the mass migration were profound. One pastor we interviewed said this:

> It was very hard to pastor a congregation – people were tired of farewell parties and it was difficult to build our church. The people in my congregation stopped connecting in relationships because it was too painful to have to say goodbye continually.

A headmaster had this to say:

> It put a huge strain on marriages. Approximately 45% of the children at school had one or more absent parents. Often both parents were out of the country working and the children were left with grandparents or older siblings. One eight-year-old girl we knew, who was being looked after by her 18-year-old cousin, was in a car accident while both parents were overseas.

Another teacher said:

> The exodus impacted the schools as they lost a lot of students. A quarter of our daughter's class left each year. As a teenager, she thought the world was going to end. We had big arguments between those who were going and those who were staying. Those who left were just so negative.

If anyone could get jobs outside the country, they generally left. This caused a huge loss of knowledge and skills in the economy and businesses suffered – those who stayed behind didn't have the opportunity to leave. They generally were unskilled and had no alternative.

Zimbabwe Diaspora: Supply from the Scattered Ones

The diaspora became a critical component of survival for those who stayed in the country. With up to one-third of the population living overseas, the influx of donations became a significant source of income for Zimbabweans – particularly donations in foreign currency, which was in scarce supply.

A host of businesses developed around this external support. Foreign exchange dealers set up offices in London and Johannesburg to facilitate transfers of money to locals. Family members sent food packs and basic necessities back home. An intricate network of distribution agents emerged.

This was the saving grace for Zimbabwe. With the need for imports far outstripping the country's capability to export, remittances of money and goods from the diaspora to their relatives was a critical source of foreign exchange, and made life more bearable. Without it, the ravages of hyperinflation would have been felt far sooner and more acutely than they were.

Pensioners: The Generation Who Lost Everything

One pensioner had to move into a tree house. He was very bright but a little bit bent. He'd climb the ladder to get to his house, but kept his books below the tree in a big plastic covering. His books were eventually eaten by ants. No one knows what came of him.

  – Social worker who dedicated her life to supporting the elderly

A discussion of the social effects of hyperinflation wouldn't be complete without referring to what happened to the elderly and retired. Over the course of a few years, the entire generation of elderly Zimbabweans were impoverished.

Hyperinflation destroyed pension savings. Those who had saved all their lives, diligently putting money into various pensions and long-term insurance schemes, lost it all. This isn't the story of one mistake of one old person; it is the story of an entire generation. The slate was wiped clean and most elderly people lost everything.

Dramatic pension losses for the elderly weren't unique to Zimbabwe's hyperinflation – this happens in hyperinflations generally. As prices accelerate higher, fixed incomes can buy less and less. By the time rampant hyperinflation arrived in Zimbabwe, a savings of Z$10 million, which was a substantial amount for a pension prior to hyperinflation, couldn't even buy a matchstick.

Old Mutual, the largest pension company in Zimbabwe, ended up gaining most of the assets that were originally allocated to pensioners. Practically, Old Mutual did everything within the law. However, the terrible effects of hyperinflation made pension assets available to the company and simultaneously impoverished a generation of elderly people.

The company now owns large amounts of Zimbabwe's commercial property, despite the fact that it doesn't owe anything on the pension obligations it had prior to the crisis. While many point fingers at the pension companies, the practical reality is that it was hyperinflation that caused this great injustice. Despite this, pension companies are a source of great resentment among Zimbabwean retirees.[36]

Most pensioners feel they were given a raw deal from Old Mutual and the other pension companies. If hyperinflation ever comes to South Africa, the UK or other countries, pensioners there can know what to expect – they can forget about any of their pension savings.

*   *   *

My dad's friend was a partner at a legal firm, having worked there for 50 years. For that entire period he had invested his retirement savings with Old Mutual. With hyperinflation, his retirement savings were decimated. Old Mutual sent him a letter saying it wasn't worth paying him monthly so they paid out the entire amount. With that payment – his entire life's pension, he bought a jerrycan of fuel.

They eventually had to sell their house, which kept them alive for three years. After that, he and his wife became destitute and had to move to South Africa to live with their son. Two years later, they both died.

Their lives petered out to a withered end. They couldn't get any medication, food or water, and few understood why their money couldn't buy anything. There were many stories of pensioners dying in their homes and many elderly couples quietly ending their lives together as they reached rock bottom.

Once, my friend gave an elderly couple a bag of 20 kilogram maize meal. At that moment, the elderly husband burst into tears. They hadn't eaten in days.

– Various comments by those interviewed

Strength in Community in a Nugget

Hyperinflation in Zimbabwe had immense social effects. One of the most notable was that it brought people together in community. Bartering, support networks and relational business thrived. Relationships were a crucial protection in the chaos of economic collapse. However, hyperinflation also slowly eroded the value system of Zimbabweans and, with it, basic trust in the society at large.

The extreme hardships of inflation caused millions to leave. Zimbabwe's scattered population – the diaspora – sent money and resources home and became a saving grace to those living in Zimbabwe.

While petty theft became much more common, violent crime was rare and mostly confined to state brutality. However, the relative lack of violent crime experienced in Zimbabwe may not necessarily be indicative of all instances of hyperinflation. In another context, violent crime may be a severe threat to survival, as it has been in other historical episodes of hyperinflation.

Lastly, while hyperinflation affected all people in society, pensioners were particularly affected. Life savings were totally destroyed, and it left millions destitute and without help. In fact, people who had diligently saved throughout their lives lost it all.

Think About It

1. Do you have a community to rely on in a time of crisis?

2. What would be the criminal response in your country to mass shortages of crucial supplies?

3. Do you rely on pension and insurance institutions to invest your money for you, and are these savings protected from high inflation or hyperinflation?

Chapter 10

The Death of the Zimbabwe Dollar

For a few years, you could find notes floating along the streets. Even the beggars didn't pick them up. They wanted clothes and food. You know your money is worthless when you see it lying on the ground.

– CEO of a manufacturing company

Making simple payments for goods and services during hyperinflation was like catching fleeing mice with chopsticks. Prices kept scampering away. Try as you might, you just couldn't pin them down.

In Zimbabwe prices rose incessantly, many times even while people stood in queues in stores to pay. Payments that would normally be a cinch to calculate became complex brain-teasers, and unique and unusual problems arose in day-to-day transactions.

Pricing Predicaments

We used to sell our sand and equipment in quadrillions of Zimbabwe dollars. No one practically knows how much a quadrillion really

*is. Have you ever heard of such a number? That is 15 zeros...15
ZEROS! How can you make a profit when inflation is so high? It all
becomes meaningless.*

– CEO of an industrial sand business

With the huge number of zeros, it became a conundrum trying to calculate
even the most basic purchases. If, for instance, you purchased six eggs, and
each egg cost Z$23 000 000 000 000, how many notes would you need if you
had denominations of Z$750 000 000 000 and Z$500 000 000? Not easy!

In particular, children and older people struggled with the calculations.
Throughout my interviews, I heard stories of pensioners being unable to
calculate payment from the money they had. Often, the elderly didn't have
the right denominations – but only found out when they got to the front
of the queues. In confusion and desperation, many would give up and leave
the stores empty-handed, if another person in the queue didn't help them.

Ordinarily simple sums, which children could calculate at lower
denominations, became very complex. Many had to shop with calculators.
Eventually the basic calculators weren't good enough – they didn't have
enough space to record all the zeros. The same applied to accounting
systems. Daily transactions couldn't be recorded electronically.

I interviewed one business owner who used an accounting system that *'could
handle transactions the size of the Russian economy'*. Even then, it couldn't
cope with the number of zeros. When the accounting systems ran out of
space for the zeros, people had to give up accounting. Many converted
their records into units of billions or trillions. But as prices accelerated
every month, it became impossible to compare monthly accounts. No
one budgeted any longer since budgets relied on a certain value of the
currency, which changed daily. Some companies turned to recording their

transactions based in an alternative metric – but those caught doing this would be jailed.

It became impossible to write out cheques properly because the space for writing was too small. The problems were the same for price tagging – often shops would leave out a zero on the price tags of various products. Astute shoppers would look for goods that were priced one zero short and quickly purchase them.

The shops had further dilemmas. Till registers couldn't calculate the transactions so the bill always had to be worked out by hand. And then each denomination of the money paid had to be counted using automated money counters. This slowed the process of trading, and queues grew longer still.

Cashiers eventually stopped using tills altogether. The number of notes coming in was far too great to be housed in tills. Instead, the money was dumped into large boxes or dustbin bags kept on the ground beside cashiers. Interestingly, we heard of no stories of these boxes ever being pinched. Money had lost its value as a target for thieves.

The Reserve Bank of Zimbabwe responded the way central banks around the world respond during periods of hyperinflation – when the number of zeros grew too great, it eventually removed these zeros from the currency. It did this three times throughout the hyperinflation, removing 25 zeros in total. To put this into context, a Z$1 note at the end of hyperinflation would have been a Z$10 000 000 000 000 000 000 000 000 note (ten septillion or ten trillion trillion) had they not removed the zeros.

'Hey, why try to calculate in trillions? Rather, remove the zeros to make it easier for everyone.' But, while this approach solved the problems posed by large denominations, it also added multiple complexities to daily transactions and accounting. It was exceptionally difficult to record transactions or have any comparable set of accounts. In one month, you may have been earning Z$1 000. And in the next month it was Z$1.

In economic terms, the value was the same because all prices also reset lower by a factor of 1 000, but it became very difficult to compare records. How does a business perform cash reconciliations with those changes? How do you work out what price is appropriate for your goods if the yardstick moves so much? First prices increase with inflation, and then prices radically fall with the zeros being removed. It put tremendous pressure on traders, which only added more fuel to the inflationary fire.

With zeros being removed, it became tremendously confusing as to which notes were applicable and which weren't, since the old money no longer applied. To combat this and to ensure a continued demand for newly printed money, the government began to put expiry dates on the notes. This made trade even more confusing for those who held expired notes. Does a note of money stop being money from one day to the next purely because it has expired? These notes continued to be traded for a while, which added to the confusion.

With inflation raging out of control, people stopped using notes and began trading in wads of cash known as *bricks*. Each brick had an approximate number of currency units in the wad, and the test for whether there were enough notes in a brick became *'if it feels right'*. The value of the bricks

themselves couldn't buy more than a loaf of bread or two, and eventually even these bricks became worthless. The value of the currency fell so far that the pulp value of the paper bricks became more valuable than the denominations themselves.

Fairly early on in the process, from around the 2003, people dispensed with using wallets or money purses, which couldn't hold the amounts of money required. Some carried their money in big brown paper bags. Others used suitcases and backpacks. For larger transactions, most used large black metal trunks.

By this stage, the Reserve Bank was printing notes around the clock – up to three million notes a day. It had been sourcing paper for its notes from the German minting company, Giesecke & Devrient, the same company that provided the notes to Germany during its hyperinflation episode in the 1920s. However, with sanctions against Zimbabwe, the company had to cease its supply, and the Reserve Bank turned to locally sourced paper, the quality of which was very poor. The falling quality of the paper only made people want to get rid of the money faster.

With the major problems in using the currency, the tide of culture began to turn against the Zimbabwe dollar and people started to use alternatives for paying and saving.

Three Alternatives to Government Fiat Money: Food, Fuel and Foreign Currency

How can you take money that is losing its value? You can't. The government was forcing us to use the paper money. It was too difficult to use Zimbabwe dollars.

— Taxi driver from Harare

As the Zimbabwe dollar became less useful to trade with, people found substitutes. The government had banned the use of foreign currency, at pain of arrest, and made it illegal to record transactions in anything other than Zimbabwe dollars. Despite this, many continued to receive foreign currency from their offshore relatives.

The economy quickly became centred illegally on a mixture of foreign currency-based trade and barter. Those who traded arrived at deal areas with their own articles of value, swapping milk for grain, or wood for water. Most of these transactions were illegal, but, out of necessity, people did it anyway.

Barter, however, can be notoriously difficult.[37] What was the swap value for each product? How much milk is needed to buy a kilogram of maize? You also had to find someone who had a product you wanted and who wanted your product at the same time.

As these barter networks became more sophisticated, a few commodities emerged as being most needed by all, and they became yardsticks in most transactions because of their high marketability. Gradually, in the most natural market-oriented way, these products morphed into alternative 'currencies' in the marketplace.

Three alternative forms of currency gained acceptance throughout the country.

1. Food money

> *The pantry was kept under lock and key because food was our equivalent currency; it was our investment and savings! We could pay for anything with our food – labour, sugar, rice, fuel etc. It was our money.*
>
> – Zimbabwean mother

Since everyone wants food on a daily basis it quickly became a highly tradable barter currency. Due to food's perishability and variable type and quality, there isn't a well-known standard of worth for 'food' as such. Nonetheless, long-lasting canned food and raw agricultural commodities were quite effective as currencies. One farmer I interviewed kept all his savings in grain and used it whenever he needed to transact with others. His barnyard was, as he called it, his *food bank*.

Businesses received food in exchange for goods and services, and lower-level staff were paid in *food boxes*. These food boxes became fairly standardised, comprising eight different items of food and basic necessities.

But with its limitations as barter currency, few large transactions were denominated in food. People had to look to more stable and uniform currency alternatives.

2. Liquid money: fuel and fuel coupons

I even paid my rent in fuel – it was a 'litre-per-square-metre' arrangement!

– Translator and teacher based in Harare

In hyperinflationary Zimbabwe, fuel was scarce because of rising demand and because it had to be imported with limited foreign currency. Electricity cuts forced many to get generators, which ran on diesel. Because of the universal demand for fuel, it was valuable both as a barter item and as a store of value. People regularly carried jerrycans of petrol to barter with, measuring out amounts and using them in trade. Very soon, other goods were priced in litres of petrol. One interviewee said it this way:

This is similar to what happens when you travel abroad and are faced with prices based in another currency. Initially, you convert prices in your head to a currency you know. But as time goes on, you get used to the local currency, and a natural switch takes place. You begin to price goods and services in the local currency. Zimbabweans started 'thinking in fuel'.

Fuel had major advantages. It was fairly uniform, and most people needed it on a daily basis to go about life and commerce. This gave fuel a unique characteristic: the government couldn't restrict it as they could foreign currency or gold, because doing so would have collapsed the economy immediately.

The government had to do something to maintain the country's fuel supply and protect the economy from instant collapse. Under great pressure, it gave a special reprieve to the fuel companies, allowing them to receive foreign currencies in exchange for fuel.

Redan Petroleum, a local fuel retailer, responded with an innovative plan. They invited people to pay for petrol and diesel in foreign currency and in return, issued a receipt known as a fuel coupon. Each fuel coupon promised to deliver at a later date 5, 10 or 20 litres of fuel.

After receiving the foreign currency, Redan sent tankers across the border to purchase fuel from neighbouring countries. When these tankers returned, people could then claim their fuel by handing in the fuel coupon at the station.

The plan was an instant success. Redan was inundated by fuel orders, and the other fuel stations quickly set up their own fuel coupon systems. With this system, the diaspora offshore could support their families by transferring foreign currency to Redan's offshore bank accounts. They would buy fuel in whatever currency they wished, and their families could access the fuel coupons. It was a smart way to send 'money' to people on the ground in Zimbabwe and avoid government regulations on dealing in foreign exchange.

While no one was allowed to hold US dollars, they were allowed to carry fuel coupons, which in the last year of inflation became a functioning alternative currency.

> *Petrol coupons were the means of currency exchange. They had a fixed value. Our legal firm was meticulous about keeping to the law. And since we couldn't use US dollars at all, we turned to receiving fuel coupons. By the end, people would bring in wads of fuel coupons as payment for our various services.*
>
> – Partner at a large legal firm in Harare

In a way, fuel companies became the new bankers. They issued 'paper money' – claims to real fuel – and became a place for people to deposit their foreign currency. None of the banking laws applied to fuel companies, which gave them considerable freedom, and by the end of hyperinflation, the economy was unofficially denominated in fuel coupons.

The fuel companies were in a powerful position. People paid them in foreign currencies and in return, they issued paper coupons with a promise to deliver fuel at a later date. However, since these fuel coupons were regarded as money and were being used in everyday payments and savings, a decreasing percentage of them were actually being redeemed for fuel.

The physical quality of the fuel coupons was poor. Many couldn't be redeemed because they became damaged or worn out. Shrewdly, the fuel companies began to add expiry dates to the coupons – if they weren't redeemed in time, they would expire. This became a source of great profit for these fuel companies since fewer coupons were being redeemed than were being issued.

Some of those interviewed said that the fuel companies increased the amount of fuel coupons relative to the amount of fuel they acquired.

They'd receive foreign currency and issue coupons, but then fraudulently not purchase fuel with their foreign currency. In other words, they were deceitfully increasing the number of fuel coupons being issued. One economist I interviewed said it this way:

> *Fiat paper currency – the currency we use today – and the current global banking system originated from a similar process. Gold used to be the most widely used form of money. However, the risk of theft was so significant that people gave their gold to goldsmiths for safekeeping in secure vaults. In return, the goldsmiths issued paper IOUs, which became like the tradable paper money that you and I know today. The goldsmiths started to increase the paper IOUs that were in issue, relative to the amount of gold that they had on hand – just like the fuel companies did in Zimbabwe. Very simply, this practice continued to the point where the goldsmiths (now the modern-day central and commercial banks) stopped holding any gold at all.*

> *Instead, the banks now take deposits of paper money. The same cycle repeats itself now, only that banks increase the number of electronic claims against this paper money, relative to the amount of paper money they hold. It highlights well the fundamental weaknesses of deposit banking: the bankers who hold money on your behalf have a perverse incentive to increase the number of claims against that money.*

By the end of hyperinflation, with the increase in fuel coupons relative to the amount of fuel that the fuel companies had on hand, the exchange value of fuel coupons had fallen by around 20%. The fraudulent increase in fuel coupons, like money printing, had caused inflation in prices denominated in fuel coupons!

Despite the benefits of fuel coupons, they had limitations as currency. As with paper currencies, the coupons were actively counterfeited. The problem got so bad that fuel companies had to introduce security measures such as holograms and unique coupon numbering. Fuel stations even resorted to taking down the personal details of everyone redeeming coupons. Fuel coupons also couldn't be used offshore. No one outside Zimbabwe would accept them in trade, so no imports could be paid for with fuel coupons. Fuel and fuel coupons were therefore a *mid-tier* currency used for most everyday transactions, but not for very large transactions or for imports.

3. 'Stable' foreign currencies

> *She hid the US dollars, South African rands and British pounds in the panelling of the door of our Isuzu truck as we crossed the border... We then discretely smuggled them across the market square in old paint tins to our rendezvous point...*
>
> – Part-time foreign exchange dealer

Large transactions were denominated in stable foreign currencies, typically by a transfer from one offshore bank account to another. Compared to Zimbabwe dollars, all other national currencies were stable and useful for trading. Yet people had to open offshore bank accounts for this, which created a host of problems, not least of which was compliance with many money laundering and banking regulations in those countries. Fortunately, Zimbabwean authorities couldn't monitor Internet transactions, so people

transferred offshore bank amounts without concerns of government snooping.

In Zimbabwe's second-largest city, Bulawayo, an informal street market for foreign currencies developed and became rather amusingly known as the *World Bank*. Numerous illicit currency dealers gathered alongside the taxi ranks. Obviously highly illegal, traders only dealt with those they knew. If you wanted to purchase foreign currency, you had to get your 'own dealer' through relational networks; most people had two or three they dealt with.

As black market trade in foreign currencies developed, the police tried to shut it down, regularly posing as dealers to catch the despised 'criminals'.

> *The way we did business was our downfall. We felt that using the black market rate was wrong because it was illegal. We were guided by our Christian faith, obeying the law and went with the existing system – not using foreign currencies at all. Later, I did a biblical study on the issue of unjust weights and measures and it changed my view on things. But that wasn't until our whole business was destroyed. We had no cashflow and couldn't import and therefore couldn't sell products. If we had used foreign currencies, our business may have survived.*
>
> – Owner of a large print company in Harare

Foreign currencies were the most important substitute for large trades. For international transactions, there were no alternatives.

Tampon Money and Other Barter Currencies

While food, fuel and foreign currency were the most important substitutes for the Zimbabwe dollar, in truth, anything that was easily tradable was useful as a form of currency to some degree.

In the women's prisons, there were shortages of tampons and sanitary pads. The demand for these was higher than for US dollars, and sanitary products soon circulated as a medium of exchange in these prisons.

People purchased cars with large cash balances just to get a hold of something that could retain its value and be resellable. Demand for new cars soared, though these cars sat idle because of fuel shortages and because they were bought to resell in good condition.

Toilet paper and cleaning equipment was also universally needed. Cell phone prepaid cards were used by some. Whiskey held its value – particularly the good quality whiskey. Others traded with old coins that retained the value of the underlying metal content.

Postage stamps were useful. They had the highest value relative to their weight, making them beneficial when transferring a large amount of value across the border. A rare stamp, the Penny Black, traded at a hefty premium in Zimbabwe, purely for its usefulness in transporting high value.

Gold and Precious Metals

As with other foreign currencies, gold and precious metals were heavily regulated by the government, and anyone caught holding gold in fairly

large amounts was arrested. All exports of any mineral ore had to be sold to the government directly at an official rate, which was hopelessly below the global market price. The black market for gold, as with all other commodities, developed around informal trading networks.

Zimbabwe has exceptionally high quality gold reserves, and many local miners had rudimentary operations to mine for surface gold. Known locally as the *skorro koza*, these local gold panners supplied wholesale dealers, who distributed it across the borders. Ultimately, the black-market operations were based around politically connected bosses who kept the police from interfering. While gold demand was high in these networks, gold was a means to obtaining foreign currencies more than using it as a medium of exchange itself.[38]

One dealer told of clandestine gold deliveries to Europe:

> *There were many people who traded gold in the underground market. I had friends who were gold couriers, carrying gold in suitcases through the airports to deliver directly to the Swiss banks. Agents from the banks would meet them directly at the Swiss airport to receive delivery. There was a 10% commission for the courier service. High, but justifiable given that they could get arrested at any time.*

The Death of the Zimbabwe Dollar in a Nugget

Hyperinflation made it very difficult to trade in Zimbabwe dollars. The rate of increase in prices and the size of the denominations created multiple complexities in everyday transactions. The complexities were compounded by the periodic removal of zeros from the currency.

The more people tried to get rid of their *scorched* Zimbabwe dollars, the more these difficulties increased. They had to find alternative ways to trade. The three most popular were food, fuel – and the associated fuel coupons – and foreign currency, each with their own set of benefits, limitations and legal sidestepping.

Other useful barter commodities were tampons, cars, toilet paper, cell phone prepaid cards, whiskey and postage stamps. Gold and precious metals played a small and limited part in trade, mostly being useful as a medium to acquire foreign exchange, or a store of value hoarded in foreign countries or in a safe place free from government confiscation.

Think About It

1. If you couldn't use the local currency in your country, what alternatives could you use?

2. How reliant are you on your national currency to perform everyday trades?

3. What would you barter with if you didn't have money?

WhenMoneyDestroys.com

PART III

Global Storm a' Brewing

"But the U.S. government has a technology, called a printing press (or, today, its electronic equivalent), that allows it to produce as many U.S. dollars as it wishes at essentially no cost. By increasing the number of U.S. dollars in circulation, or even by credibly threatening to do so, the U.S. government can also reduce the value of a dollar in terms of goods and services, which is equivalent to raising the prices in dollars of those goods and services."

> – **Ben S. Bernanke**, Remarks before the National
> Economists Club, Washington, D.C. November
> 21, 2002

In Part I, we explained the big picture of hyperinflation as it was seen in Zimbabwe's economy. Part II then looked at the practical effects of hyperinflation in the everyday lives of people in Zimbabwe and how they survived.

In Part III, we apply the principles learned from Zimbabwe to a global context. Governments of the world's major economies are highly indebted and are increasingly making the political move to print money on a large scale to fund expenditure. Building on Chapter 4, we identify the warning signs of potential currency crises and hyperinflation in the world's most developed economies, particularly in the global financial hub, the United States. We end by looking at ways to prepare and respond constructively to such potential threats.

Chapter 11

Dollar Supremacy

Let me issue and control a nation's money and I care not who writes the laws.

— **Mayer Amschel Rothschild**

As of 2015, the US dollar is the global reserve currency. What does that mean? In short, it means that most countries in the world opt to keep a large portion of their savings in US dollars and to conduct international trade with US dollars. But how did the US get such an important role in global trade?

1944–1971
Bretton Woods

America emerged from World War II as the global superpower with most of the world's gold reserves. In 1944, towards the end of the war, the Allied forces met together to establish a financial system that became known as the Bretton Woods System. In essence, America would keep the vast majority of the world's gold – the internationally accepted money at the time – and the rest of the world would trade in US dollars as a substitute for gold. If any foreign government ever wanted to redeem gold with the US dollars it held, it could do so in New York with the Federal Reserve at US$35 per ounce. It was agreed that the Federal Reserve would always keep sufficient gold in its vaults to facilitate the redemption of paper dollars. In other words, dollar notes were actual ownership certificates for real gold vaulted in the US. In addition, all other countries agreed to keep a roughly fixed amount of their own currencies relative to the number of dollars they held, in order to maintain fixed exchange rates.

With the major trading powers all using the US dollar, it became the standard currency for most of the Western world. It was used as the basis for trade between countries, and if countries had cash surpluses, they would store them in US dollars by reinvesting back into America, keeping them in 'reserve'. Although these reserves were investments in the United States, most countries believed that they were indirect claims to real gold.

This put America in a tremendously advantageous position. Similar to how the Zimbabwean fuel companies had the ability to create fuel coupons during Zimbabwe's hyperinflation, America over time increased the number of US dollars relative to the amount of gold it held. By the late 1960s, America was in a costly war in Vietnam and government welfare expenditures were swelling. The Federal Reserve and the US banks began to print dollars to pay for these expenses. Countries that exported products to America had to make real goods and services with inputs of labour and materials, and in return they were paid in money that was created out of nothing. This started off slowly at first but gathered momentum throughout the 1960s.

By the early 1970s, a few countries began to realise that there were more US dollars in circulation than gold held by the US – if all the major Bretton Woods members decided to claim gold from the Federal Reserve with their US dollars, there would not be enough gold for the amount of dollars that were in circulation. France and Switzerland in particular began to get

in line to sell large amounts of dollars for gold. What started off as a few gold redemptions at the Federal Reserve gathered pace. If the countries of the world realised that the dollar was no longer '*as good as gold*', perhaps they would stop holding it as reserve currency. America's global financial influence would be dealt a severe blow. As far as America was concerned, something had to be done urgently.

1971–1981
The Nixon Bomb: The Gold Window Closes

And so came the fateful day on 15 August 1971 when President Richard Nixon announced that the US would no longer convert dollars into gold. Foreign countries that held dollars now couldn't legally claim their gold, and America could print money without worrying about losing 'America's' gold reserves.

Since paper dollars had under the Bretton Woods System been ownership certificates to real gold in the vaults of the Federal Reserve, Nixon's closing of the gold window amounted to a major default by America on its international obligations.

With no fixed backing, the value of the US dollar began to plummet. By the end of 1972, the gold price had doubled, from US$35 per ounce to US$70 per ounce, meaning the value of the dollar had halved in just one year. With the dollar's value in freefall, prices rose higher and higher all over the world. Inflation was accelerating, and trust in the US dollar was waning fast.

For the previous 27 years, the world had given America the right to print money in return for real goods and services. Now America faced the risk that this right could be taken away, with predictably painful consequences. Control over the levers of international trade and finance was at stake, and pressure was mounting. Global markets were building up to a decisive moment. Then, in January 1973, the US stock market crashed.

The precursors to hyperinflation that we studied in Part I were unmistakable. The US had been overspending on wars and welfare initiatives. The closing of the gold window and the subsequent stock market crash were various 'Black Friday' turning points as formerly complacent investors began pulling back their loans and investments. The signs were pointing towards a hyperinflationary spiral and America desperately needed to find ways to keep the world using its currency.

Facing potential economic turmoil, at the end of 1973, Nixon's administration struck deals with Saudi Arabia and other nearby oil-producing states of the Middle East to sell oil exclusively in exchange for US dollars and to invest their excess dollar profits back into America by lending to the US government.[39] In return, these countries would get a steady supply of the latest US weapons and US military protection for their oil fields from potential invaders like the Soviet Union. By 1975 most of the other major oil-producing countries had also agreed to this plan.

The arrangement created a triangular flow of investment that gave the United States a powerful double subsidy. Those purchasing oil had to purchase US dollars first. The oil-selling country then had to reinvest those dollars into the US.

From an American perspective, the plan was a political and economic masterstroke. Since everyone needed oil, countries that saved surpluses in US dollars could then fund oil purchases. The dollar remained a paper currency with no tangible backing, yet demand for it was strengthened by the global oil trade, which was growing rapidly. This arrangement gave rise to the name *petrodollars*, which described the intimate link between the dollar and oil. It took a few years for countries around the world to gain confidence in the dollar again, but by 1981, the petrodollar system, as it became unofficially known, had helped firmly re-establish the US dollar as the global reserve currency.[40]

1981–1999
Dollar Dominance

The petrodollar system spread beyond the realm of oil. Since everyone now needed US dollars, other international transactions became denominated in US dollars. Everyone who wanted to trade between countries first had to accumulate US currency, keeping these US dollars invested and easily accessible. The most accessible way was to lend them to the US government by purchasing US bonds. With so many available investors, the American government had the ability to run up immense debts.

Economists call this arrangement America's '*exorbitant privilege*', and it's hard to find a better description for the financial sweet-spot America found itself in.[41] After the tumultuous 1970s, the US dollar reclaimed its global financial supremacy, allowing Americans to buy imported goods at a huge discount and consume well in excess of their means.

The entire global banking system became structured around the US dollar. In time, the Federal Reserve, the International Monetary Fund and the World Bank became established as the chief regulators of the system.[42] Since most international loan transactions were denominated in US dollars, these three organisations could, and did, come to control international finance.

1999–?
Dollar Under Threat

About trade settlement, we have decided to use our own currencies …

– **Vladimir Putin**, Russian president discussing
Russian-Chinese trade

Despite support for the petrodollar system, the European Union (EU) also wanted the *exorbitant privilege* of a reserve currency. EU leaders began to look for ways to create a centralised European currency that could compete with the US dollar for global trade and reserves.

The discussion evolved into a reality, culminating in what became known as the Euro Project. In January 1999, the euro as a currency was introduced, and it quickly increased in status. Countries in and around Europe began saving in euros, and trade with the EU came to be denominated in euros instead of US dollars. Euros began to compete with the US dollar as a global reserve currency.

With the euro's increased status, demand for the currency grew, and there was rapid growth of investment into Europe. Since the ultimate goal of the euro project would be to rival the US dollar in the oil trade, the main oil-producing countries began discussions with Europe over a potential

186

petroeuro project. In November 2000, Iraqi President Saddam Hussein began selling oil to Europe in euros,[43] and in 2002 OPEC speculated:

> *It is quite possible that as…trade increases between the Middle East and the European Union, it could be feasible to price oil in euros, considering Europe is the main economic partner of that region.*[44]

Later Syria overtly rejected the dollar as a reserve currency and began to trade in euros,[45] while some Eastern European countries, including Russia, began to hold larger euro reserves than dollar reserves.

If other currencies were to be used in payment for oil, demand for US dollars could fall. The *exorbitant privilege* America had enjoyed over the years with its money as the global reserve currency would disappear if its currency monopoly ended.

Petrodollar Wars

> *We gradually stopped using Zimbabwe dollars. The only way they could keep us using it was by force – gently massaging us with the barrel of a gun.*
>
> – CEO of a Zimbabwe fabrics factory

The petrodollar system, and particularly the vested interests in sustaining it, is probably *the* critical issue in global geopolitics today. Said simply,

America has everything to lose if nations of the world use other currencies in trade. These are powerful vested interests to protect. Viewed through this lens, recent global events take on a new light.

Petrodollar Wars – Iraq

The US invasion of Iraq was ostensibly about disarming the Saddam Hussein regime of its weapons of mass destruction. No such weapons were ever discovered, and many commentators have suggested that America was actually interested in Iraqi oil supplies. Yet, buying oil peacefully from Iraq would have been a much easier and cheaper way to get oil.

Until November 2000, no oil-producing country had dared violate the petrodollar pricing arrangement, and while the US dollar remained the strongest currency in the world, there was little reason to challenge the system.

In late 2000, the European Union, spearheaded by France, convinced the Iraqi leader, Saddam Hussein, to denominate the sale of Iraq's oil in euros rather than US dollars. This opened the discussion for many other countries to consider doing the same. Russia and Iran were both very interested in this option. Finally, in April 2002, a representative of OPEC's oil cartel met with the European Union to discuss how at some point they could sell oil to the European Union denominated in euros. American 'concerns' regarding weapons of mass destruction in Iraq coincided with these petroeuro talks. Just under a year later, the United States invaded Iraq.

The German and French governments were vociferous in their opposition to the invasion – they knew the consequences of euro-denominated oil trade. Sure enough, shortly after the invasion, the United States quickly re-established the dollar pricing rule for Iraq's oil sales.

Petrodollar Wars – Iran

Very similar dynamics have been at play with Iran. Talks to investigate currency alternatives to the US dollar in exchange for its oil started shortly after the creation of the euro currency and by 2005, the Iranian government announced its intent to develop an Iran Oil Bourse – an oil-trading platform that would allow anyone to purchase oil in a number of alternative currencies, other than the US dollar.

It was an important project since there were no internationally recognised exchanges that provided competitive euro-based oil pricing. Conventional exchanges, such as the Norway Brent Crude or the West Texas exchanges, dominated global oil sales – each with dollar pricing.

By the end of 2007, shortly before the opening of the exchange, Iran had met with the largest Japanese and Chinese oil purchasers and had secured their involvement in purchasing with alternative currencies.[46] The trading platform was moving ahead, despite US resistance, and officially opened in February 2008.

In the years that followed, America increased its pressure on Iran, ultimately instituting sanctions against the country in 2010 for its supposed development of nuclear weapons. The US was so vociferous in its sanctions pressure that it threatened any country or bank trading with Iran with total exclusion from the global banking system if they were caught facilitating purchases of Iranian oil.[47]

The threats were exceptionally effective and global trade with Iran fell dramatically. The effect on Iran was crippling. Its government turned to money printing to continue funding its expenses, leading the country down the path towards a currency crisis and potential hyperinflation.

Petrodollar Wars – Libya

Libya has the largest proven oil reserves in Africa. Its eccentric leader, Muammar Gaddafi, was against what he termed 'US imperialism' and became interested in aspects of the Murabitun World Movement, a discussion relating to the reintroduction of the gold dinar, the currency of the Muslim world until the collapse of the Ottoman Empire in 1924. He began to lobby for a 'gold-for-oil' programme with which to trade Libyan oil on global markets, in particular between other Arab and African countries.

The Guardian, on the subsequent Libyan civil war, reported:

> ...he initiated a movement to refuse the dollar and the euro, and called on Arab and African nations to use a new currency instead, the gold dinar. Gaddafi suggested establishing a united African continent, with its...people using this single currency. During the past year, the idea was approved by many Arab countries and most African countries. The only opponents were the Republic of South Africa and the head of the League of Arab States. The initiative was viewed negatively by the US and the European Union, with French President Nicolas Sarkozy calling Libya a threat to the financial security of mankind; but Gaddafi was not swayed and continued his push for the creation of a united Africa.[48]

The country had 100 tons of existing gold reserves with which Gaddafi was going to trade. He didn't get to implement his plan, however. In 2011, an anti-Gaddafi uprising broke out. The rebel forces, funded and militarily backed by America, the chief power behind the NATO invasion, took over the country and killed Gaddafi.

NATO had declared a 'no-fly zone' over the country to stop Libyan bombings of rebel strongholds, which US Defence Secretary Robert Gates described in his speech to a US House Appropriations Committee:

> *A no-fly zone begins with an attack on Libya to destroy the air defences. That's the way you do a no-fly zone, and then you can fly planes around the country and not worry about our guys being shot down.*[49]

The US-led offensive was particularly brutal, bombing most of the Libyan defence infrastructure and Gaddafi's private dwellings, as well as inflicting extensive collateral damage in the capital city of Tripoli. The United States and European governments seized Libyan national overseas investments and supplied weapons to the rebel forces.

Then, one month after the start of protests, the rebel groups announced the creation of '*the Central Bank of Benghazi as a monetary authority competent in monetary policies in Libya and appointment of a Governor to the Central Bank of Libya, with a temporary headquarters in Benghazi.*'[50]

That was quick. When last did rebel groups made up of mercenaries, farmers, teachers and other civilians set up a fully functioning central bank while fighting for their lives in a civil war – and that within one month of the start of the conflict?

A week after the announcement, the US declared that it would accept the sale of oil from rebel leaders only, despite official sanctions against the country. Through the newly controlled oil companies and central bank, the oil sales gave the rebels a much-needed US$100 million, and more importantly, ensured Libyan compliance in the petrodollar system.[51]

The evident protection of the various vested interests was instrumental in the overthrow of the government and subsequent assassination of Muammar Gaddafi. It maintained the denomination of Libya's oil sales in US dollars and the recycling of Libyan dollar profits back into the United States.

Other Petrodollar Pressure Points

The recent global diplomatic pressure on Russia regarding Ukraine appears to be influenced by these same petrodollar vested interests – Russia has been openly talking about de-dollarising its trade and instituting the Russian ruble as an alternative, particularly in its gas trade with its European customers.[52]

China, too, has ambitions for global reserve currency status, and it has launched a trading platform to allow countries to purchase oil in Chinese yuan.[53] China is a major military power, which makes it difficult for America to restrict its currency ambitions through military force.

China and Russia in particular have led the anti-dollar agenda, creating in 2010 the first yuan trading platform outside China and Hong Kong on

the Moscow Interbank Currency Exchange and announcing that bilateral trade between the two countries would be settled in Russian roubles or Chinese yuan, not US dollars.[54] China has made similar strides with Japan, one of its largest trading partners.

Since at least 2008, China has been taking ever more active steps to 'internationalise' the Chinese yuan. The People's Bank of China, China's central bank, has signed a host of bilateral currency swap agreements with foreign central banks. The purpose of these agreements is to reduce the US dollar denominated trade between China and other countries, using yuan and other currencies instead. It is part of China's strategy to encourage its trading partners to hold more yuan in reserve to pay for goods from China.

China has made bilateral currency swap agreements with the likes of South Korea, Malaysia, New Zealand, Australia, Turkey, UAE, Brazil, United Kingdom and the European Union.[55]

Meanwhile, Brazil, Russia, India, China and South Africa, collectively known as the BRICS, have openly pledged to work towards building a BRICS development bank to perform the traditional roles of the IMF or World Bank, except that it would extend financial assistance in currencies other than the US dollar.[56]

It is not surprising to see American antagonism towards Russia escalating to the point of sanctions ostensibly over territorial sovereignty disputes thousands of miles away from Washington. Expect ongoing tension between the US and Russia as the latter further tries to cut the dollar out of international trade and financial relations.

Reserve currency ambitions aren't new. Even small regional powers such as South Africa try to influence their surrounding countries to use their currencies as benchmarks, in the hope of obtaining special money printing privileges.

America's number one geopolitical imperative is maintaining its exorbitant monetary privilege. The same goes for the Eurozone. As these currencies are printed on a large scale, they have had to resort to increasing force and control to maintain their reserve currency status.

Dollar Supremacy in a Nugget

In 1944, the US dollar became the main currency to be used in trade by the Western world, under an arrangement known as the Bretton Woods System. It envisaged a fixed peg of dollars against gold and all other currencies against the dollar. By 1971, the number of dollars in the system had increased beyond what America could possibly facilitate if countries redeemed their dollars for gold, and Nixon had to close the gold window. This amounted to a major default by the United States. The US government worked in tandem with oil-producing countries to establish the petrodollar system – global oil trade based in US dollars – which maintained the dollar as global reserve currency despite no gold backing. This put America in a powerful position of *exorbitant privilege*. The United States has a tremendous amount to lose if this privilege is challenged. To compete for global transactions, the European Union created the euro currency, while China also desires reserve currency status for its currency, the yuan.

Reserve currency vested interests are massive. At stake is America's *exorbitant privilege* to print its money, knowing that others will take printed money in exchange for real goods and services.

As in Zimbabwe, when a government has made the political decision to print money on a large scale, it has to increase its control over the population to get them to continue using that money. Petrodollar wars – the recent wars in Iraq and Libya, and the sanctions against Iran and Russia – are potential examples of this on an international scale. Nations around the world are scrutinising the US dollar's status as global reserve currency and are placing increased pressure on the petrodollar system. Where this pressure leads to will be a defining characteristic of global geopolitics over the next several years.

Think About It

1. Why do you use the money you use? What makes you ascribe value to it?

2. What is the real difference between counterfeit pieces of paper that pose as money and real pieces of paper that circulate as money? Why does the one have value and the other doesn't?

Chapter 12

Total Transaction Control

No one believes more firmly than Comrade Napoleon that all animals are equal. He would be only too happy to let you make your decisions for yourselves. But sometimes you might make the wrong decisions, comrades, and then where should we be?

— **George Orwell**, Animal Farm

Power tends to corrupt and absolute power corrupts absolutely.

— **Lord Acton**, 1887

For decades now, governments of the United States, Japan, Britain, continental Europe and many others have gorged themselves on debt. Since the banking crisis of 2008, these countries have spun into a vicious debt spiral not very different from the early stages of Zimbabwe's financial malaise.

They've all made the political decision to print money to continue funding their excesses. To delay the negative effects of money printing for as long as possible, they've had to increase control over financial systems – commonly

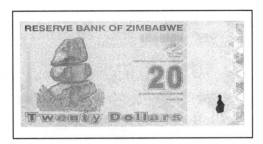

known as *financial repression*, institute trade restrictions, and compel the population to use the money and keep prices low – what we know as *transaction control*. There is a grave risk that transaction control will lead to totalitarianism and the associated loss of freedom for ordinary citizens.

We focus in this chapter on the United States, since the US dollar is the global reserve currency. However, these trends are common in other countries as well.

Alphabet Surveillance

The more a society monitors, controls, and observes its citizens, the less free it is.

– Benjamin Franklin

A government can control people's transactions only to the extent of its surveillance and intelligence gathering. In Zimbabwe, the relative lack of sophistication in its government surveillance techniques limited its ability to control. The opposite is the case in America. The federal government is bent on acquiring as much information as possible through a program originally coined as *Total Information Awareness*,[57] which started from as early as 2001. Because the dollar is effectively the world's currency, as US-based money printing increases, America would need to exert transaction control globally, not just on its own citizens.

Over the years, it has created 16 'alphabet soup' agencies from seven different US departments that form the Intelligence Community. These include the CIA, DIA, NSA, NGA, NRO, AFISRA, INSCOM, MCIA, ONI, OICI, I&A, CGI, FBI, DEA/ONSI, INR and the TFI.[58] Those are a lot of agencies trying to track your information, and they have the tools they need to do it.

Recently, the Intelligence Community opened a vast data warehouse in Utah called the Intelligence Community Comprehensive National Cybersecurity Initiative Data Centre that can store over a yotabyte of data (a thousand trillion gigabytes). It sweeps most of the world's Internet data from undersea cables and the servers of major multinational Internet companies. The goal is to store all worldwide electronic information flow comprehensively for further data analysis.

On top of this, the programs X-Keyscore and Fairview focus on accumulating international information, searching, analysing and storing Internet data and the mobile phone metadata of foreign nationals. Cell phone metadata includes your geographic movements and details of all the phone calls you've made, as well as all your text messages. In addition, in specific countries under surveillance, it records *all* phone calls.

The Intelligence Community has further developed a computer virus known as Magic Lantern that logs all your keystrokes, allowing the FBI to decrypt your communications, passwords and other sensitive information. It also has a program that can perform instant wiretaps on any telecommunications device located in the United States. A program, Boundless Informant, gathers other Internet data. Almost three billion data units from the United States were recorded in March 2013 alone.[59]

Together these programs capture the important telecommunications and computer data of all the citizens in every country in the world. That

includes you. They do this by working in conjunction with other foreign intelligence agencies and through multinational telecommunication agreements.

> *The NSA partners with a large US telecommunications company, the identity of which is currently unknown, and that US company then partners with telecoms in the foreign countries. Those partnerships allow the US company access to those countries' telecommunications systems, and that access is then exploited to direct traffic to the NSA's repositories.*
>
> – **Glenn Greenwald**, journalist for The Guardian60

Private Companies Get in on the Act

The data-sweeping programs have legal jurisdiction over the major privately owned Internet companies with access to much of their information. These companies – Microsoft, Apple, Dropbox, Google, AOL, Facebook, Amazon, Twitter and Yahoo – effectively control global access to the Internet, including access to online VoIP services, cell phone operating systems, cloud-based services, Internet searching, map analysis and a host of other critical Internet applications.

Add the various telecommunications companies, and combined, the close relationship they have with the US and other governments gives the Intelligence Community sweeping, nearly total access to information about you and your transactions.

Other Intelligence Gathering

The information gathering is increasing in pace. Alarmingly, a Biometric Optical Surveillance System (BOSS)[61] has been developed that recognises faces on photographs and can identify individuals in a crowd. Now, all CCTV recordings of you anywhere, together with all your public photos, can be scanned by supercomputers and stored electronically.

The Intelligence Community also has an encryption breaking program known as Bullrun. Reporting on it, *The Guardian* said:

> *Those methods include covert measures to ensure NSA control over setting of international encryption standards, the use of supercomputers to break encryption with 'brute force', and – the most closely guarded secret of all – collaboration with technology companies and internet service providers themselves.*[62]

Even your encrypted information is no longer private.

The deep intrusion on personal privacy isn't unique to America. The Intelligence Community works closely with Australia, Canada, New Zealand and the United Kingdom in an intelligence-sharing agreement known as the *Five Eyes*. The UK can, for example, spy on American citizens and make that information available to the US government on its enormous, NSA-operated spy cloud.[63] The German intelligence service is said to be targeting the same level of surveillance as its American counterparts.[64]

These many different spy programs are using all surveillance means possible to gain *total information awareness*. You can be assured in the

knowledge that almost all of your movements and social interactions are being recorded.[65]

Regulatory Overload

> *Those who are capable of tyranny, are capable of perjury to sustain it.*
>
> — **Lysander Spooner**, nineteenth century philosopher

In Zimbabwe, the government passed a labyrinth of laws designed to increase the reach of the state into everyday private life.

And as with Zimbabwe, the quantity of American laws, rules, and regulations has been quite simply exploding. CNN reported that 40 000 new laws would take effect in 2014 alone in the United States.[66] There are about 80 000 pages of detailed government regulations in the *Federal Register*, which excludes by-laws, departments, agencies, and regulations at the state and local level, up a staggering 300% since 1970.[67]

Since the 2008 financial crisis, legislative bills have ballooned in size. The Dodd-Frank financial regulation bill, signed into law in 2010, was a gargantuan 850 pages long, generating by 2014 just over 14 000 additional pages of rules and regulations, written by six federal agencies, pertaining to its implementation.[68] Another example is the Patient Protection and

Affordable Care Act, also know as *Obamacare*, which is nearly 1 000 pages long and had by 2014 generated over 11 000 pages of implementation rules.[69] In January 2014 the US Congress passed a government spending bill that was 1 600 pages long – a bill that most legislators admit to not even having read in full.[70]

In a world of increasing transaction control, there is – as in Zimbabwe – a proliferation of laws giving government the power to rule by decree.

Financial Totalitarianism

Control of the financial system is an important part of any transaction control program. The United States has almost complete worldwide control over currency and global banking. For example, the same threat that was effective in forcing sanctions against Iran was just as effective against Wikileaks. After the organisation leaked numerous classified documents, the United States cut off Wikileaks' access to banking services. No one could transfer any money to Wikileaks via conventional banking channels.

The Intelligence Community has access to vast amounts of global financial information. The US Treasury collects and analyses financial transactions in conjunction with another intelligence program that accesses the global clearing house of international transactions: the SWIFT database.

The major credit card companies are all based in America: Visa, MasterCard, American Express and Discover (which owns Diners Club). Combined, they cover almost all global credit card transactions.

Cell phone companies are quickly moving into the credit card space with Apple leading the way with its Apple Watch and iPhone payment systems. Cellphone companies and the various banks are partnering to provide mobile money alternatives, which are rapidly accelarating around

the world. Further, the various credit card and banking companies are all introducing smartphone payment apps. Since every phone delivers a constant tracking signal via the cellular data networks, this convergence of payment and cellular provides a unique tracking technology that monitors both your payments and your geographic location.

Mechanisation of Control

> *The Homeland Security Department wants to buy more than 1.6 billion rounds of ammunition in the next four or five years…about the equivalent of five cartridges for every person in the United States.*

> – The Denver Post, February 2013

For a government to control transactions at home and around the world, it needs to exert ever greater levels of military and police control – just as Zimbabwe did. In the United States, the police are arming up. Homeland Security is purchasing all forms of military-style armoured vehicles and tanks for local law enforcement. The same goes for most other developed countries. Here are just some of the latest unclassified weapons available to the US government.

High Energy Beams

The Vehicle-Mounted Active Denial System[71] is a supposed 'non-lethal' beam with a range of 700 yards and can render any group of resisters powerless within milliseconds. It works using microwave technology that causes its victims to feel excruciating pain all over their skin. Overexposure leads to severe burns. It also superheats any metals within range, making it impossible for you to hold on to any metallic equipment during exposure to the ray.

Drones and Creepers

Most countries are fast developing their own drone technologies. More than 57 countries have developed various unmanned aerial vehicles (drones); from 2013 onwards, each of these countries has been engaging in an international robotics arms race. America is currently winning the race with its drones and unmanned ground vehicles (creepers).

In addition to the well-known Predator-type drones, the US military has developed a host of mini surveillance drones that match nature's flying birds and insects, one such being the RoboBee.[72] Further research is being conducted into arming these miniature robots with the latest chemical and biological weapons. The US military has developed advanced systems to automate these flying robots in swarms, which defy the best anti-aircraft weaponry available.[73] There are also large blimp-type drones that can 'see in 360 degrees over a 340 mile distance'[74]

When it comes to creeper technologies, there are some bizarre and frightful advances. The Big Dog is a four-legged rough-terrain robot that walks, runs, climbs and carries heavy loads. And then there is the Sandflea (which jumps over 30-foot walls), the RiSE (which climbs vertical surfaces) and, perhaps most alarmingly, a terminator-style walking humanoid known as the Atlas.[75] These are a handful of thousands of different robotic applications currently under development. Robotics has come a long way but the technologies will advance much further in power, stealth, surveillance and firepower over the next few years. In the shadow of all this, your guns are... well...so 1980s.

Drones may provide authorities with powerful additional surveillance options to monitor the movements of everyone, in addition to enforcement options. Linked in with cell phone and payment convergence, the technology is available for each person to be constantly monitored, watched and controlled. It is not hard to imagine that as governments print money excessively, cell phone, credit card, biometric identification and drone technologies could converge into one technology that enables government to enforce *total transaction control*.

Total Transaction Control in a Nugget

If a government is printing money on a large scale, it would need to control its population simultaneously to ensure that the money it is printing is used and that prices are kept low, which we call *total transaction control*. This is achieved through *total information awareness*, increased policing, advanced military technology, extensive surveillance and legislative reach – which have all made *total transaction control* imminently achievable and something money printing governments can resort to.

Think About It

1. Do you have the technology to communicate securely and privately?

2. How could you transact efficiently yet without being monitored?

3. If demanded, is it wrong to refuse to hand over your private information to the government?

Chapter 13

Get Prepared

I was now resolved to do everything in my power to defeat the system.

— **Oskar Schindler**

My uncle was concerned about the money printing in the country so he researched other hyperinflations in South America. With this information, he developed innovative strategies that made him financially very successful. His business did very well because of his research.

— Young Zimbabwean waitress

How would you protect and provide for yourself and your family during hyperinflation?

In a money printing world, this book should be fuel to the fire of your own research, education and sense of responsibility. The Internet is rich with good material, from further explanations of the economic risks we face to practical survival strategies during a breakdown of trade and social order. In researching the experience of Zimbabweans, we learned some critical insights that we share below.

Get Out While You Can

We missed Zimbabwe terribly. But life changed so quickly for us and for the better when we left. A lot of people battled with the final decision of leaving. But we were so glad when we left. We should have done it much earlier. We were nomads away from our home country but were much safer than if we had stayed...

– Zimbabwean father of three based in Botswana

The best way to survive hyperinflation, without a doubt, is to avoid it completely. For the roughly four million who left Zimbabwe, life improved in an instant. No longer were there extreme shortages of everything, and political, financial and social pressures were relieved. We know that this isn't something that can be advocated for all people, but based on the responses of Zimbabweans we interviewed, it is certainly an important consideration if hyperinflation ever becomes a serious risk in your country.

Do you have an emigration plan? Have you considered getting a second or third passport or contacting emigration specialists for advice? It isn't easy to uproot and leave family and community networks. Emigrants tend to struggle financially and lack social support structures, but, as many Zimbabweans have highlighted, this pales in comparison to the hardship of living through hyperinflation.

Leaving may also be restricted by the government. Monitoring and restriction of movement at border posts would likely increase during times of acute economic crisis. The Zimbabwean government didn't have much ability to stop those fleeing, but if they could, they probably would have.

Relational Wealth

We stayed – it just wasn't easy to uproot. We had to look after each other. We all had a tremendous sense of gratitude and open-heartedness for the support that each person gave.

– Zimbabwean family

If you decided to stay, the only way that you would survive hyperinflation would be through relationships and community. Zimbabweans became more dependent on one another under the pressure of food shortages and crime. If you were a loner, your chances of survival were slim.

You may consider doing a lifestyle audit to assess which goods are most important and how you would source these. The best solution during hyperinflation is to engage with your community to barter for the goods you need. Existing social organisations have an advantage. In Zimbabwe, as the pressure on society increased, country clubs, alumni organisations, churches and charity clubs quickly became centres of support and trade. Access to supplies was based purely on relationships, and trust was a crucial alternative to money.

In addition to supplying key goods, community also offers protection. What would it look like in your own country if shops emptied, water supplies dried up and prices soared? As social safety decreases, there is increased protection in close communities.

Zimbabweans benefitted from the large diaspora that helped them by sending home goods and stable currencies. This community abroad was a critical component of survival.

During hyperinflation, as your ability to rely on money disappears, a deep and connected community around you would be a key survival strategy.

You would have to seek this out as a deliberate focus. Who would you be able to trust in dark times?

Think About the Morality of Law

If he was a virtuous, honest guy, no one in a corrupt, greedy system like the SS would accept him...Schindler used corrupt ways, creativity and ingenuity against the monster machine dedicated to death.

– **Zev Kedem** about his World War II saviour

In Part II we referenced a Christian woman who felt obliged to obey the law because of her faith, even in the face of extreme injustice.[76] She faced a moral dilemma. Although she disagreed with the laws that brought her to poverty, she felt a moral obligation to obey them. This would be a terrible dilemma for any of us. When the laws of the land become corrupt, coercive, and inhibit our ability to survive, very often breaking them is the only sensible option to take, despite the risk of penalty. Which laws remain good and which are corrupt? With some laws, it's easy to tell, but with others, the line is blurred.

In Zimbabwe, the government became increasingly despotic as money printing spiralled out of control. The law became centred on furthering the government's selfish interests and its control – very different from any sense of just morals and ethics. By the end of hyperinflation, trust in the justice of the law had evaporated.

To survive, you would need to separate the two concepts of legality and justice. Nelson Mandela and Mahatma Gandhi were both great leaders in resistance movements against corrupt and totalitarian government regimes. They taught people not to comply with unjust laws. Ultimately, these are profoundly personal decisions that each person living under hyperinflation needs to make.

The Zimbabweans we interviewed had this to say:

> *Hyperinflation is a hideous scenario because it brings out the worst level of government control and manipulation and the depravity of human nature is exposed.*

*   *   *

> *If you stay in your country, you need to come to terms with the moral dilemmas embedded in a system that is geared towards deep and fundamental corruption. This is no ordinary decision. Would you live in a system that is inherently structured to reward the corrupt and penalise the just? If you choose to stay living in such an awful scenario, you would have to consider whether you have the ability, with integrity, to get politically connected.*

*   *   *

> *There are hundreds of politically connected elite in Zimbabwe who have to live with the reality that millions live in poverty (and indeed many people died) because of their prosperity.*

Learn How to Listen

Governments use confusing language and rhetoric as a powerful tool of control. You should learn how to understand statements made by the authorities. Learn what they are saying and specifically what they are *not* saying. Practically, most things aren't too complicated for the average person to understand, despite what many governments (and economists) would have you think. A useful rule of thumb is this: If you don't understand what they are saying, it probably means they don't want you to understand.

Business Techniques in Hyperinflation

The primary purpose of this book isn't to highlight business strategies in hyperinflation[77]. At a very high level, however, there are some important principles to consider in relation to the changing business environment during hyperinflation.

Managing Assets, not Earnings

In Chapter 5 we described what happens to businesses during hyperinflation. The challenges for companies are manifold, including soaring input costs, price controls, restrictions on foreign currency ownership, difficulties in paying staff, dealing with failing municipal services, and coping with falling demand for products and services as people become poorer or leave the country.

In such adverse operating conditions, businesses must change how they think, away from a customer-oriented paradigm to a survival paradigm. In this process, conventional profits diminish in importance. Instead, companies must focus far more on owning tangible assets and tradable goods that are durable and marketable enough to act as stores of value. A good way to do this would be to evolve from providing a particular good or service to managing assets or becoming a trader.

Key considerations here include trying to anticipate the risk of the government taking the assets you hold and trying to keep abreast of a rapidly evolving and tightening regulatory environment. For this reason, owning assets in foreign countries that respect property rights could be a sound strategy. Companies would more than likely have to make tough choices around tough questions. Would you break petty regulatory rules to survive? Would you engage in black market trade?

Alternatives to Banking and Money

As money becomes less useful, you would need to find alternatives. As a government prints lots of money, it would likely try as hard as possible to restrict any currency other than the state-sanctioned currency. Money has a few important uses. It is a store of value, a medium of exchange and a mechanism to invest/ lend. It is also a measure for people to be able to record transactions. You would need to find alternatives for each of these core functions of money.

1. Store of value

As much as you can, you should consider, during a period of very high inflation or hyperinflation, allocating a proportion of your savings offshore and denominated in stable currencies and assets. With many countries in the process of printing money, it isn't all that clear which currencies are preferable. You would need to assess which countries have more or less risk to your own. Since all governments have the ability to print paper currencies, the best alternatives are likely metallic or commodity forms of money. Gold, silver and fuel are currencies that cannot be 'printed' or increased on a large scale.

2. Medium of exchange

How would you pay for goods and services without using your national currency? There are a number of gold transaction platforms available that have some attractive transaction services. However, if the government controls the Internet and payment networks, your options may become limited. Internet security may also be an issue with online payment platforms. The same applies to investments and lending. Cryptocurrencies (encrypted online digital currencies) such as Bitcoin may offer sufficiently secure, anonymous and convenient ways to transact. These technologies are evolving quickly, and it would be important to keep abreast of the latest advances and innovations in these electronic currencies. These technologies are in their infancy – like computers were in the 1970's – and may well fashion the future of money and banking as existing payment systems deteriorate with large-scale money printing programs.

3. Unit of account

If you can't benchmark, how can you possibly know what your margins are?

— CEO of a large Zimbabwean importing firm

In a hyperinflationary environment, those who run businesses would need to find a way to record transactions based on a stable measurement. They would need to find a yardstick of value. It must be a relatively stable benchmark for recording transactions and ideally be used by other businesses as well. In Zimbabwe, people used all kinds of yardsticks, from fuel to food parcels, and gold to US dollars. One economist, Jonathan Waters, even developed the 'hard-boiled egg index' to obtain a more accurate measure of inflation and the exchange rate from what was reported in official statistics. This index became quite popular, even in banking and financial circles.

Pensions

Hyperinflation reduces almost all pensions savings to nothing, even large amounts saved in the pension funds. Expect that your pension investments would either be reduced to nothing or nationalised.

A financial advisor in Zimbabwe had this to say:

> *If I was advising Zimbabwean pensioners prior to the country's currency collapse, I would have said the following: Cash in your pension policies. If you are on a pension, move it into something worthwhile. Pension schemes will not remedy themselves – if you have any fixed income positions they will reduce to nothing in hyperinflation. You need to go against all Western views of savings and storing money in cash and bonds. Convert all of your cash and savings into things that store value and in things that you will need to survive. Both government and private pensions will not save you.*

Exports Denominated in a Stable Currency

The premium placed on foreign currency during hyperinflation makes export industries relatively very profitable. There are numerous aspects to consider in exporting effectively in a depreciating currency, but the most important is to ensure that your exports are denominated in a stable foreign currency – a currency that isn't losing value rapidly, which is widely trusted and which operates within a banking system that facilitates international transfers. During hyperinflation, governments typically try to expropriate foreign earnings so you would need to consider the numerous ways to get around that risk, possibly by holding most funds offshore and only repatriating the minimum amount needed to operate.

Debt

Debts denominated in a hyperinflating currency quickly become worth next to nothing. Borrowers are usually able to pay back debts with ease while lenders are paid back in money with a lower purchasing power than it had when they lent it. Typically, interest rates can never appropriately compensate for hyperinflation, so those who get access to loans (and who can make the repayments) benefit tremendously.

However, you should consider the personal ethics of borrowing during hyperinflation. If you borrowed from banks, you would be aiding the inflation process by acquiring loans of newly created credit money. You would be complicit in the destructive effects of money printing and no longer clearly be able to distinguish yourself from the system that created the problem in the first place. You'd be an integral part of the problem.

If you borrowed from people or businesses outside the banking system, you would be faced with another challenging question. Is it right to borrow from others, expecting they would be ruined by hyperinflation? Is it an honourable, fair trade to make? Would you borrow from a relative or friend in this way?

A common issue pertaining to the dilemma around law and ethics highlighted earlier in this chapter is deciding whether or not to disobey the law. But equally there are times when you may have to assess whether you should refrain from doing something you are permitted to do. Borrowing money in expectation of hyperinflation may be one such case.

Borrowing and lending in a stable currency could continue and indeed thrive. For example, it might be that you could get a loan denominated in gold, fuel or food. In Zimbabwe, this happened often with fuel and foreign currency (it's how the fuel coupon system became more widely used). Lending in stable currencies protects the lender so the borrower can borrow with a clear conscience.

Cash

If hyperinflation became an imminent risk, you would need to consider whether to take your money out the bank. Once you had the cash in hand, you would have to try buying something that would last and could be easily traded in the near or distant future – for example, foreign currencies, gold and silver coins, fuel or durable food. Very high bank deposit interest rates during hyperinflation create the impression that your money in the bank is 'growing'. This is an illusion. The real purchasing power of cash in the bank falls rapidly towards zero. At this point, cash is neither a reliable unit of account nor a safe store of value – it is only a medium of exchange and therefore should only be held for very brief periods to facilitate trade.

Save and Invest Now

If you took your funds out of the formal investment sector, you would still be faced with the question of where and how to save. This is a complex question that we cannot deal with sufficiently here. It is clear that going into hyperinflation with no savings in real assets or stable alternative currencies is a major disadvantage. Being diversified in your savings is important. Traditionally, during times of high inflation or hyperinflation, people sought protection in things as diverse as company stocks, precious metals, property, rare collectors' items and trusted foreign currencies. However you choose to save, each asset should be assessed based on its proven ability to store value, how easy it would be to sell in a time of great need, how costly it is to transport, protect and maintain, and how safe it is from government confiscation and a crashing economy.

If you try to avoid debt, have you considered ways to buy expensive assets without debt, such as saving first in affordable assets that will hold their value during inflation, or finding partners who can co-own assets with you?

Consider spending time and effort, seeking advice, deciding whether you save enough and planning how and where you want to save.

Are you investing your time and energy in building strong relationships with friends and family? Your networks and relationships become invaluable 'savings' during an economic crisis.

Get Prepared in a Nugget

You need to be sober about the risks of hyperinflation and take ownership of the responsibility to protect yourself and your family. The easiest survival technique in hyperinflation is to leave. You would need to consider the impact of hyperinflation on all aspects of your life if you decided to stay or weren't able to leave, including food, goods, water supply, and municipal and corporate services. You would also need to find alternative commodities to trade in.

From a business perspective, you would have to consider building a good quality base of durable, marketable assets. This includes getting your money offshore in stable currencies and commodities such as gold and silver, purchasing 'hard assets' and benchmarking your business against stable yardsticks. Look to export and get out of any loans you've made. Make sure you don't hold more cash than is absolutely necessary to make certain important transactions.

Think About It

1. What level of government coercion or economic mismanagement would cause you to consider leaving your own country?

2. What would your response be if you were faced with the moral dilemma of obeying the law or feeding your family?

Chapter 14

Your Opportunity

The Chinese use two brush strokes to write the word 'crisis'. One brush stroke stands for danger; the other for opportunity.

– John F Kennedy

The only thing more daunting than an economic crisis is coming out of the crisis having learned nothing, doomed to repeat the mistakes of the past. Sadly, the problems in Zimbabwe teach us that life doesn't get much better after an economic crisis unless corruption and government control are flushed out and society is reorganised justly. Years after the end of hyperinflation in the country, it is still languishing in economic malaise and poverty.

> *Reset is the word. Hyperinflation was terrifying before the currency reset. But things changed greatly on the other side of it. Life and systems looked different. We had to look at our relationships and community structures all over again. They changed. You need to know what it is that you are changing to and how you will make those changes.*
>
> – Zimbabwean political commentator

What does it look like after a currency has gone through hyperinflation and finally collapsed? The answer depends on the choices that a society and its leaders make to influence their country towards a positive reset.

Solutions for Fixing the System

Those from among you will rebuild the ancient ruins; You will raise up the age-old foundations; And you will be called the Repairer of the Breach...

— Isaiah 58:2

While it is important to find solutions to problems found during hyperinflation, our first task is to understand their root causes, which has been the goal of this book.

Often when we understand what causes the problem in the first place, the essence of the solution becomes self-evident. For example, if deficit spending and money printing ruin economies, we should establish a system that removes the state's ability to go into debt and to control and print money. In the unnecessary complexity of modern economic jargon, the obvious problems with money printing and excessive debt have become blurred in society's consciousness. This is the reason we have focused so much on this problem in this book — to highlight the simple cause and effect of poor decisions and the political structures that allow them.

The historical evidence is clear. For any country to correct itself from currency collapse, both deficit spending and money printing need to end. It is the pressure placed on government by excessive debt obligations that ultimately drives money printing. However, the knowledge that it can simply print money also emboldens government to spend and borrow too much. Government debt and money printing are self-perpetuating twin injustices that lead to economic ruin – both need to be ended. This was highlighted in a definitive paper written by Nobel Prize-winning economist, Thomas Sargent, where he analysed the outcomes of four large inflations in the early twentieth century.[78]

Powerful vested interests benefit from money printing and debt-fuelled consumption, largely because of society's ignorance. Yet, as these injustices are laid bare to ordinary people, there is a critical window period for learning and reform.

What, then, are the best structures to facilitate a sound and just money system?

We strongly advocate that as a foundation, people must have freedom to choose whatever money they wish to use in trade. This means that legal tender laws that 'lock' people in to using only one currency controlled by the government should be repealed. Money and different money alternatives should be services offered by competing enterprises, in the process decentralising the power and privilege associated with money and its creation. When the government has monopoly control over the money supply, there are few checks on its power to increase the amount of money in the system fraudulently. We therefore advocate allowing the markets to define currency naturally, and legal structures that let people trade in whatever money they choose.

The only standard needs to be one of justice. If an organisation says that the money it issues has a certain backing, such as oil or gold, it must actually have that backing. The money must be what it says it is. At its basic root, this is about trading honestly. The full extent of government involvement in money should *only* be to ensure that issuers of currency maintain honest money – money that is what it says it is.

In order to allow people the freedom to choose their own money, banking and financial structures need comprehensive reform. A system of privately produced competing currencies should be subject only to ordinary commercial law – there would be no need for a central bank or any other authority with the power to exact monopoly control over money production. Banks in turn would no longer have the privilege of accessing newly printed money in the form of central bank loans and bailouts. They would have to run their businesses responsibly, and if they incurred losses, they would have to look to private shareholders for bailouts, or declare bankruptcy – just like any ordinary business. Banks would have to focus on finding people willing to save money with them by building trust and a sound business track record, rather than accessing special money printing privileges.

Likewise, clearing houses for payments between banks (which in our current day are facilitated and controled by the central banks) should be privatised, and based on the prepayment of reserves – with cross-banking clearing performed based on known existing money stores held within the clearing house.

Many national currencies are linked to vulnerable reserve currencies, such as the US dollar. Unless these links are severed, they will share the fate of those reserve currencies. In the 1920s, Austria, Hungary and Poland failed to de-link their currencies sufficiently from the collapsing German mark and got pulled into their own hyperinflation crises. National paper currencies need to be linked to a sound backing, such as gold and silver; have legal tender monopoly removed and be opened up to face competing currencies.

The underlying cause of hyperinflation is excessive government spending that precedes money printing. Governments should therefore have strict constitutional limitations on their ability to tax, spend and borrow.

Those who pay tax should be allowed to do so in any of the major private currencies in use.

It's not just about respecting private property rights in money, but *all* private property rights. Hyperinflationary crises fundamentally change the character of society and relationships. Family, friends and community structures are crucial to stable social order, particularly in times of societal reform. We advocate the importance of private property and land ownership within families and communities instead of putting these things into the hands of government. Private property ownership, particularly as it relates to money, has been shown to be a pillar on which to build successful, ordered communities.

Opportunity

Economic crises are usually associated with great wealth transfers and new opportunities. In Zimbabwe, those who were prepared for what was to come were able to protect their wealth and build upon new opportunities. Collapsing municipal services provide opportunities for smart entrepreneurs to provide those services privately. Society's shifting values in a time of crisis places much more emphasis on certain products and services than others, creating new business opportunities in a host of products, services, sectors and industries. Tremendous opportunities exist in helping facilitate trade. Obtaining access to productive farm land, fresh water sources or fuel supply channels can also lead to significant opportunity as demand for basic necessities skyrockets. Harnessing smart, affordable energy solutions that reduce or eradicate reliance on the municipal grids can become a major business opportunity.

Technology can also be a game changer. Online cryptocurrencies and related services can provide tremendous benefit as paper currencies collapse. Specialist mobile apps that create solutions to people's everyday problems are a huge untapped opportunity, such as allowing community networks to connect, communicate, and coordinate transactions and supply logistics, or helping people work out and pay for goods and services in high and fluctuating complex currency denominations. The potential technological solutions in a time of great crisis are practically endless.

*　　*　　*

The lessons from Zimbabwe's struggles are clear. When nations enact irresponsible economic policies and then print money to fix their problems, the inevitable result is economic ruin. This pattern has been repeated over and over in history, always with the same results.

It requires maturity to face risks honestly and to respond with clear purpose, rather than to recoil in fear. In many senses, the good news is that you now know the bad news! You have the ability to respond to the challenges only when you understand them. The opportunity you have is to help bring about constructive change, and that starts in your own life, then in your family, your community, your work environment and beyond. This is your opportunity.

When Money Destroys Nations: Nugget o' Nuggets

Since the financial crisis of 2008, the major governments of the world have resorted to printing large amounts of money to pay national debts and bail out banks. The warning signs are clear, and Zimbabwe's experience of rampant money printing is a useful guide to what lies in store if urgent and painful reform is not enacted. Prior to its hyperinflation, Zimbabwe was loaded with economic potential. It had abundant infrastructure and trade was booming – yet the country marched towards hyperinflation with a series of poor economic decisions.

For years Zimbabwe's government borrowed excessively to pay for war and welfare entitlements, culminating in the Black Friday crash in 1997. International lenders withdrew funding, forcing Zimbabwe into a debt spiral. The government responded by printing money to pay its debts, pushing Zimbabwe down a perilous inflation gorge.

As inflation accelerated, the Zimbabwean government had to increase its control over the population to monitor transactions and to plunder the nation's assets. It fiddled with inflation statistics and used obscure language to conceal the true nature and extent of its money printing. A host of new laws were enacted, particularly in controlling bank transactions, prices and everyday trade. The state increased the police and military presence, and the justice and penal systems were skewed heavily in favour of the ruling party. The media and local centres of influence were infiltrated and controlled.

Finally, in 2008, 11 years after the Black Friday crash, the Zimbabwe dollar collapsed in a heap of worthless paper.

What *is* hyperinflation? It is the dramatic process of an established currency losing its usefulness as money. Prices rise rapidly and uncontrollably as a result of excessive money printing and a loss of confidence in the currency.

Money printing causes a rise in prices known as inflation, which over time creates a *culture* of inflation. As money printing accelerates, so do rates of inflation. People expect prices to rise at an increasing rate and begin to seek refuge from rapidly rising prices by getting rid of money as fast as they can and buying real things that hold value.

At this stage, people don't want to trade in the currency and only do so under the compulsion of legal tender laws and government force. Most local businesses go under. A time comes when no one, not even the government, wants to use the currency any longer, and it collapses. The economy goes through its final and inevitable contraction. At this point, people turn to alternative, stable currencies, and the country is forced to rebuild its economy and society from ground zero.

Hyperinflation is the ultimate in economic chaos and disorder, leaving in its path economic ruin. The toll of human suffering in Zimbabwe was immense. Living standards plummeted. Basic services disintegrated. Stores emptied. Food, water and other necessities that people took for granted became incredibly difficult to find. Government services collapsed and municipalities went bankrupt. Experienced and skilled staff left in droves. Systems broke down and important equipment deteriorated.

Hyperinflation forced communities closer. Bartering, support networks and relational business helped people survive. However, the extreme economic injustices meant desperation set in, slowly eroding the deep integrity of the Zimbabwean people and, with it, their trust in the community. The elderly suffered terribly. Their savings were destroyed and they were left destitute.

Millions left Zimbabwe with little hope of ever returning. They sent money and resources home to those who stayed during the worst period of hyperinflation, and some continue to support those friends and loved ones even to this day.

Violent crime, except that perpetrated in the name of politics, never became a major problem during hyperinflation. This is a great testimony to the patience and peacefulness of Zimbabweans.

It was a colossal challenge to trade in Zimbabwe dollars, with the rate of price increases and the size of the transactions creating brain-shuddering complexities in everyday affairs. People found currency substitutes, the most useful of which were food, fuel and foreign exchange. These evolved into unique currencies with different strengths, weaknesses, and functions.

Other useful barter commodities were tampons, cars, toilet paper, airtime, whiskey and postage stamps. Gold and precious metals played a small but limited part in trade, mostly being useful as a medium to acquire foreign exchange. As always happens during chronic currency debasement, gold and silver were driven out of circulation as people hoarded these valuable metals in an attempt to store wealth.

Zimbabwe contains lessons for the global economy. The US dollar is the global reserve currency resting on the back of the petrodollar system. There are deep-rooted and enormously powerful vested interests keeping people trading with US dollars – yet today, numerous other powers are threatening to diversify trade away from dollars to reduce this currency hegemony. At stake is America's *exorbitant privilege* – its ability to print money out of nothing in exchange for real goods and services from the rest of the world. Like Zimbabwe, the American government has made the political decision to print money on a large scale, meaning it likely will have to increase its control over the population to keep them using that money. *Total transaction control* is a tremendous risk to personal economic freedom as governments print money.

Money printing and the collapse of confidence in your nation's currency may be the greatest risk – and the greatest opportunity – you could face in your life. You can learn from those who've gone before.

Make sure you are prepared.

Endnotes

1   http://www.businessweek.com/articles/2013-09-12/
    hank-paulson-this-is-what-it-was-like-to-face-the-financial-crisis#p4

2   http://www.businessweek.com/articles/2013-09-12/
    nancy-pelosi-on-getting-the-tarp-votes-to-save-the-economy

    http://www.independent.co.uk/news/business/news/paulson-was-
    down-on-one-knee-begging-for-a-deal-944046.html

3   Technically quantitative easing and other money printing
    programmes don't actually print physical money. While money
    printing is a part of the process of increasing the money supply, the
    vast majority of money is 'created' by digital accounting. This reflects
    on bank accounts but there is no physical underlying money – it is,
    in essence, electronic money. The money in banks is mostly numbers
    on a computer. The effect, however, is exactly the same as printing
    money. Using its unique and special legal privilege, the Federal
    Reserve creates money out of nothing and purchases government
    bonds and mortgage-backed securities, many of which have no value.
    The result is basically the same as giving it to the banks directly.

    By buying US government bonds the Federal Reserve, in an indirect
    but very real way, gives the government newly printed money to fund
    its expenses.

    Central banks aren't the only ones to print new money. When
    commercial banks get money from the central bank, they multiply that

amount of money, not by printing, but by lending out much more than they actually have on hand. They do this by simply recording on your bank statement that you have the money deposited with them when they lend it to you. When people like you and I get a loan from the bank, the bank doesn't actually have most of the money. The bank has essentially 'created' electronic money through loans which exceed their actual cash holding. A common term for this kind of money is 'bank credit money'.

This process has, in its current form, been going on since 1971 as part of the flexibility that banks and central banks have in the post-gold-standard system. However, with the massive bank debts and government financing required, quantitative easing has accelerated this process and has resulted in large increases in money printing.

[4] http://data.worldbank.org/indicator/CM.MKT.LCAP.CD

[5] http://object.cato.org/sites/cato.org/files/pubs/pdf/workingpaper-8.pdf

[6] In its colonial days, Zimbabwe was known as Southern Rhodesia and subsequently the Republic of Rhodesia after the Unilateral Declaration of Independence of 1965. For a brief six-month period from June 1979 it was named Zimbabwe-Rhodesia. The end of the peace treaty in December 1979 saw it revert to the pre-UDI name of Southern Rhodesia until the country was finally named the Republic of Zimbabwe after independence in 1980.

[7] For further reading on the causes of other hyperinflationary episodes, read the paper 'The Ends of Four Big Inflations' written by Thomas Sargent in 1982.

ENDNOTES

8   http://www.imf.org/external/pubs/ft/wp/2013/wp13266.pdf

9   Raftopoulos, Brian and Mlambo, Alois (eds). *Becoming Zimbabwe: A History from the Pre-colonial Period to 2008*. Johannesburg: Jacana Media, 2009.

10 http://mises.org/journals/qjae/pdf/qjae14_3_3.pdf

11 Dollarisation was the moment of the collapse of the Zimbabwe dollar and the acceptance of other currencies as alternatives. It occurred between November 2008 and February 2009. In November, the government gave numerous shops special licences to trade in US dollars. By the end of January, other currencies had obtained legal tender status, and by 3 February 2009, anyone could legally refuse to accept Zimbabwe dollars. Within a few days, Zimbabwe's currency was dead.

12 2012 Mid-term Monetary Policy Statement by the Reserve Bank of Zimbabwe Governor Dr. G. Gono: http://www.rbz.co.zw/pdfs/2012%20MPS/Mid%20Term%20MPS%20July%202012.pdf

13 http://www.whitehouse.gov/sites/default/files/omb/budget/fy2015/assets/28_1.pdf

14 http://www.ssa.gov/budget/

http://www.ssa.gov/policy/docs/statcomps/supplement/index.html

http://www.irs.gov/uac/
SOI-Tax-Stats-Individual-Income-Tax-Returns

15 http://www.federalreserve.gov/releases/z1/current/

[16] http://www.iea.org.uk/publications/research/a-bankruptcy-foretold-2010-post-financial-crisis-update-web-publication

http://www.ecb.europa.eu/pub/pdf/scpops/ecbocp132.pdf

http://www.ncpa.org/pdfs/st319.pdf

http://www.bis.org/ifc/events/2011_dublin_111_06_hagino.pdf

[17] St. Louis Federal Reserve, Federal Reserve Economic Database

[18] http://www.bloomberg.com/news/2013-11-20/pboc-says-no-longer-in-china-s-favor-to-boost-record-reserves.html

[19] The increase in M1 money supply (which is made up of notes and coins in the hands of the public and demand deposits – digital money – in bank accounts) in Zimbabwe from 1990 was much more than the major economies after the banking crisis of 2008. This is a key factor in delaying the loss of confidence in the major currencies currencies and subsequent high inflation.

[20] http://www.mckinsey.com/insights/economic_studies/debt_and_not_much_deleveraging

[21] US Department of the Treasury: Financial Management Service

[22] The US Federal Reserve expanded its balance sheet assets (a measure related to the money supply) by nearly 40% in 2013 and by 350% since 2008. The Bank of Japan also grew its balance sheet by 40% in 2013 and has doubled it since the financial crisis. The Bank of England has expanded its balance sheet by 300% and the European Central Bank balance sheet grew by 50% since 2008.

ENDNOTES

23 http://www.europarl.europa.eu/news/en/
news-room/content/20131212IPR30702/html/
Deal-reached-on-bank-%E2%80%9Cbail-in-directive%E2%80%9D

24 http://recoveryandresolutionplans.wordpress.com/2013/10/03/
banking-reform-bill-bulks-up/

25 http://larouchepac.com/dodd-frank

26 http://www.budget.gc.ca/2013/doc/plan/budget2013-eng.pdf (pp
144–145)

27 http://finance.yahoo.com/news/banks-in-europe-are-charging-to-
hold-deposits--could-it-happen-here-195532627.html

28 http://www.ecb.europa.eu/pub/pdf/scpops/ecbocp132.pdf

29 http://www.bloomberg.com/news/2010-11-25/hungary-follows-
argentina-in-pension-fund-ultimatum-nightmare-for-some.html

http://pensionsandsavings.com/pensions/
pole-axed-pensions-politicians-raiding-pensions-again/

30 http://investmentwatchblog.com/the-feds-us-land-grab-hidden-
within-purchase-of-mortgage-backed-securities/

31 The final moments of the burning balloon and subsequent crash were caught on a mobile phone camera by a nearby tourist, and the video went viral on YouTube.

32 In 1956, the economist Phillip Cagan wrote 'The Monetary Dynamics of Hyperinflation'. His definition of the moment hyperinflation starts

is in the month that the monthly inflation rate exceeds 50%; it ends when the monthly inflation rate drops below 50%, and stays that way for at least a year. Annualised, this is 12 874% per year. By his own admission, the 50% threshold is arbitrary. However, this is the figure that most of the academic community embrace as a definitive moment when a country enters hyperinflation.

The International Accounting Standards Board makes reference to a rate but also lists factors that indicate the existence of hyperinflation:

- The general population prefers to keep its wealth in non-monetary assets or in a relatively stable foreign currency. Amounts of local currency held are immediately invested to maintain purchasing power;
- The general population regards monetary amounts not in terms of the local currency but in terms of a relatively stable foreign currency. Prices may be quoted in that currency;
- Sales and purchases on credit take place at prices that compensate for the expected loss of purchasing power during the credit period, even if the period is short;
- Interest rates, wages and prices are linked to a price index; and
- The cumulative inflation rate over three years approaches or exceeds 100%.

[33] Many scholars also call this *malinvestment.*

[34] Some economists translate Mises' German phrase *Katastrophenhausse* as the *Crack-up Boom.*

[35] See the Cato Institute's Troubled Currencies Project (http://www. cato.org/research/troubled-currencies-project) for the difference

between the black market and the official exchange rates reported by government – evidence of how governments understate the extent of currency depreciation during a currency crisis.

36 This was the general consensus view of those we interviewed. We contacted the Africa division of Old Mutual in Johannesburg highlighting our findings to give them a chance to respond – they declined to comment.

37 The main problems with barter are:

- *Double coincidence of wants*: It is rare that both people want what the other has. Adam Smith, the so-called father of modern economics, described the problem of barter as the '*double coincidence of wants*';
- *Absence of common measure of value*: It is difficult to know what the exact exchange amount for each barter transaction is. Normally we denominate transactions in one common currency. In barter, there is no standard denomination;
- *Indivisibility of certain goods*: Sometimes a person only has a large indivisible item to barter (such as a house or a car) and can't barter for a smaller value of another good;
- *Difficulties in debt*: Because there is no standard denomination, it is difficult to handle deferred payments or loan transactions; and
- *Difficulty in storing wealth*: Very often, barter transactions are done with things that are perishable – such as grain or milk.

38 Gresham's Law states that people will hoard good money and get rid of bad money by trading with it. This was certainly the case in Zimbabwe. Gold and other precious metals were not used in exchange but instead were hoarded as a store of wealth and value, to be sold only if necessary to survive.

39 In practice, Saudi Arabia invested any excess profits in US Treasury bonds, notes and bills. In other words, this increased loans to the United States government. This became known as dollar recycling, and as this new system became entrenched, the recycled dollars were made available to US banks and the World Bank. The history to this is discussed in detail in the book *Petrodollar Warfare* by William Clarke.

40 After the petrodollar system was established, global investors remained sceptical that the dollar could survive unbacked by gold. They continued to sell dollars for gold in the late 1970s, and the gold price soared. By 1981, a decade after 'The Nixon Bomb', the gold price had rushed to $800 per ounce. In just ten years of being unbacked by gold, the dollar had lost 95% of its value.

In the final act of America's dollar restoration plan, Federal Reserve Chairman Paul Volcker drastically slowed the supply of new money by raising short-term interest rates to almost 20%. This did three important things. First, it made it more expensive to borrow from American banks, so bank lending, and hence bank money printing, slowed down. Second, it encouraged Americans to save money because they earned more interest on their savings. More savings were therefore made available to fund investment projects that began to make America more productive. Third, it made it much more attractive for foreign countries to invest their cash surpluses in US government bonds because they earned more interest doing so.

It had the desired effect. The dollar stabilised and then began strengthening. The gold price fell rapidly. America had convinced the world to use a dollar unbacked by gold.

41 The term *privilège exorbitant* was first coined by Valéry Giscard d'Estaing, the French finance minister in the 1960s, referring to America's ability to finance its trade deficit using its own currency.

42 The International Monetary Fund (IMF) was set up under the Bretton Woods system. It served as a global policeman, 'helping' member countries keep fixed exchange rates by giving them short-term dollar loans to manage exchange rates.

From there, the World Bank was established. It mainly took deposits from the US and lent them to countries needing long-term loans, denominated primarily in US dollars. As the petrodollar system grew, the World Bank took in recycled dollars from oil-producing countries. These two organisations have been pivotal in establishing global dollar supremacy.

43 http://www.rferl.org/content/article/1095057.html

44 OPEC, the Organization of the Petroleum Exporting Countries, is a cartel of oil-producing countries that operate together to influence prices and limit the supply of oil in the market. You can find the discussion to use the euro as petrocurrency here: http://www.opec. org/opec_web/static_files_project/media/downloads/publications/ OB042002.pdf

45 http://news.bbc.co.uk/2/hi/business/4713622.stm

http://www.bloomberg.com/apps/news?pid=newsarchive&sid=axsVay f83Ow4

46 http://www.nytimes.com/2007/03/27/business/worldbusiness/27iht-euros.1.5042807.html?_r=0

47 By this stage, the US had almost complete control over the global banking system: credit card networks, the SWIFT international payments system, and the Bank of International Settlements.

48 http://www.theguardian.com/commentisfree/cifamerica/2011/apr/21/libya-muammar-gaddafi

49 http://www.cnn.com/2011/US/03/02/libya.military.options/index.html?_s=PM:U.S.

50 http://www.thenewamerican.com/world-news/africa/item/8318-libyan-rebels-create-central-bank-oil-company

51 http://www.reuters.com/article/2011/03/28/us-libya-oil-rebels-idUSTRE72R6X620110328

52 http://www.vestifinance.ru/articles/42686

53 http://www.examiner.com/article/dollar-no-longer-primary-oil-currency-as-china-begins-to-sell-oil-using-yuan

54 http://www.chinadaily.com.cn/china/2010-11/24/content_11599087.htm

55 http://www.bloomberg.com/news/2013-10-10/ecb-sets-currency-swap-line-with-pboc-as-euro-china-trade-rises.html

http://en.wikipedia.org/wiki/Internationalization_of_the_renminbi

http://www.forbes.com/sites/jackperkowski/2012/06/26/china-busy-signing-currency-deals/

56   http://www.reuters.com/article/2013/09/05/
us-mp-g20-brics-idUSBRE9840E020130905

57   The Electronic Privacy Information Centre gives an in-depth discussion
regarding the *Total Information Awareness* program at http://epic.org/
privacy/profiling/tia/. The comments are from March 2005.

58   As of 2014, the 16 intelligence agencies that are part of the United
States Intelligence Community (IC) are:

1.   Independent agencies
1.1. Central Intelligence Agency (CIA)
2.   United States Department of Defense
2.1. Defense Intelligence Agency (DIA)
2.2. National Security Agency (NSA)
2.3. National Geospatial-Intelligence Agency (NGA)
2.4. National Reconnaissance Office (NRO)
2.5. Air Force Intelligence, Surveillance and Reconnaissance Agency
      (AFISRA)
2.6. Army Intelligence and Security Command (INSCOM)
2.7. Marine Corps Intelligence Activity (MCIA)
2.8. Office of Naval Intelligence (ONI)
3.   United States Department of Energy
3.1. Office of Intelligence and Counterintelligence (OICI)
4.   United States Department of Homeland Security
4.1. Office of Intelligence and Analysis (I&A)
4.2. Coast Guard Intelligence (CGI)
5.   United States Department of Justice
5.1. Federal Bureau of Investigation (FBI)
5.2. Drug Enforcement Administration, Office of National Security
      Intelligence (DEA/ONSI)
6.   United States Department of State

6.1. Bureau of Intelligence and Research (INR)

7.   *United States Department of the Treasury*

7.1. Office of Terrorism and Financial Intelligence (TFI)

[59] http://www.theguardian.com/world/2013/jun/08/
nsa-boundless-informant-global-datamining

[60] http://www.theguardian.com/commentisfree/2013/jul/07/
nsa-brazilians-globo-spying

[61] http://www.nytimes.com/2013/08/21/us/facial-scanning-is-making-
gains-in-surveillance.html?pagewanted=all&_r=0

[62] http://www.theguardian.com/world/2013/sep/05/
nsa-gchq-encryption-codes-security

[63] http://www.theguardian.com/commentisfree/2013/jun/13/
prism-utah-data-center-surveillance

[64] http://www.theguardian.com/commentisfree/2013/oct/04/
german-intelligency-service-nsa-internet-laws

www.stiftung-nv.de/mstream.ashx?g=111327&a=1&ts=63516935687
1880160&s=&r=-1&id=152076&lp=635162174190900000

[65] Glenn Greenwald has written a detailed book revealing the scope of
NSA surveillance. Published in 2014, it is called *No Place to Hide:
Edward Snowden, the NSA, and the U.S. Surveillance State* and is
published by Metropolitan Books

[66] http://thelead.blogs.cnn.com/2013/12/31/40000-new-laws-take-
effect-in-2014/

ENDNOTES

67 https://www.federalregister.gov/uploads/2013/05/
    FR-Pages-published.pdf

68 http://www.davispolkportal.com/infographic/july2013infographic.
    html

69 http://obamacarefacts.com/obamacarebill.pdf

70 http://rules.house.gov/bill/113/hr-3547-sa

71 http://www.globalsecurity.org/military/systems/ground/v-mads.htm

72 http://motherboard.vice.com/blog/
    the-worlds-smallest-robot-is-a-drone

73 http://rt.com/news/us-drones-swarms-274/

74 http://www.cnbc.com/id/102303444#.

75 http://www.bostondynamics.com

76 Gary North deals with the Christian ethics of money printing and
    banking in his excellent book, *Honest Money*. Further details can be
    found at our website: *WhenMoneyDestroys.com*.

77 We provide personalised advisory services to support and develop
    businesses as they deal with the risks and opportunities faced
    in hyperinflation. If you are looking for strategies to profit in
    hyperinflation or protect your business, investments or pensions, go to
    WhenMoneyDestroys.com for further information.

78 http://www.nber.org/chapters/c11452.pdf

List of acronyms

AFISRA	Air Force Intelligence, Surveillance and Reconnaissance Agency
AIG	American International Group
ASPEF	Agricultural Sector Productive Enhancement Facility
ATMs	Automated Teller Machines
BOSS	Biometric Optical Surveillance System
BRICS	Brazil, Russia, India, China, South Africa
CCTV	Closed-Circuit Television
CEO	Chief Executive Officer
CGI	Coast Guard Intelligence
CIA	Central Intelligence Agency
CNBC	Consumer News and Business Channel
CNN	Cable News Network
DEA	Drug Enforcement Administration
DIA	Defence Intelligence Agency
DRC	Democratic Republic of Congo
EU	European Union
FBI	Federal Bureau of Investigation
GDP	Gross Domestic Product
I&A	Office of Intelligence and Analysis
IMF	International Monetary Fund
INR	Bureau of Intelligence and Research
INSCOM	Army Intelligence and Security Command
LED	Light-Emitting Diode
M1	Broad Money Supply
MCIA	Marine Corps Intelligence Activity
NATO	North Atlantic Treaty Organisation
NECI	National Economic Conduct Inspectorate

NGA	National Geospatial-Intelligence Agency
NGO	Non-Governmental Organisation
NRO	National Reconnaissance Office
NSA	National Security Agency
OICI	Office of Intelligence and Counterintelligence
ONI	Office of Naval Intelligence
ONSI	Office of National Security Intelligence
OPEC	Organisation of the Petroleum Exporting Countries
PAYE	Pay As You Earn
QE	Quantitive Easing
RBZ	Reserve Bank of Zimbabwe
SWIFT	Society for Worldwide Interbank Financial Telecommunication
TARP	Troubled Asset Relief Program
TFI	Office of Terrorism and Financial Intelligence
UAE	United Arab Emirates
UDI	Unilateral Declaration of Independence
UK	United Kingdom
US	United States
ZESA	Zimbabwe Electricity Supply Authority

List of Big Numbers

One	1
Thousand	1000
Million	1 000 000
Billion	1 000 000 000
Trillion	1 000 000 000 000
Quadrillion	1 000 000 000 000 000
Quintillion	1 000 000 000 000 000 000
Sextillion	1 000 000 000 000 000 000 000
Septillion	1 000 000 000 000 000 000 000 000
Octillion	1 000 000 000 000 000 000 000 000 000
Nonillion	1 000 000 000 000 000 000 000 000 000 000
Decillion	1 000 000 000 000 000 000 000 000 000 000 000

Bibliography

Bernanke, Ben S. 'Japanese Monetary Policy: A Case of Self-Induced Paralysis?' For presentation at the ASSA meetings, Boston MA, 9 January 2000. December 1999.

Bernholz, Peter. *Monetary Regimes and Inflation*. Massachusetts: Edward Elgar Publishing, 2003.

Braun, Eduard. 'The Subsistence Fund in Ludwig von Mises's Explanation of the Business Cycle' in *Theory of Money and Fiduciary Media: Essays in Celebration of the Centennial*. Auburn Alabama: Ludwig von Mises Institute, 2012.

Bresciani-Turroni, Costantino. *The Economics of Inflation* (English translation by Millicent E Sayers). North Hampton: John Dickens & Co Ltd, 1968.

Cagan, Phillip. 'The Monetary Dynamics of Hyperinflation' in Milton Friedman (ed.), *Studies in the Quantity Theory of Money*. Chicago: University of Chicago Press, 1956.

Calvo, Guillermo. 'Puzzling Over the Anatomy of Crisis: Liquidity and the Veil of Finance'. Background paper for the Mayekawa Lecture at the Institute for Monetary and Economic Studies Conference, Bank of Japan, Tokyo, Japan, 29–30 May 2013.

Clark, William. *Petrodollar Warfare*. British Columbia. New Society Publishers, 2005

Coomer, Jayson and Gstraunthaler, Thomas. 'The Hyperinflation in Zimbabwe'. *The Quarterly Journal of Austrian Economics*, Vol. 14, No. 3, Fall 2011, 2011.

Cope, Landa. *The Old Testament Template*. The Template Institute Press, 2006.

Dem, Amadou, Mihailovici, Gabriela and Gao, Hui. *Inflation and Hyperinflation in the 20th Century – causes and patterns*. Columbia University, 2001.

Denver, The Post. Homeland Security aims to buy 1.6 billion rounds of ammo. *The Denver Post*.

15 February 2013. Fergusson, Adam. *When Money Dies*. London: William Kimber, 1975.

Fergusson, Adam. *When Money Dies*. London. William Kimber, 1975.

Gokhale, Jagadeesh. *Measuring the Unfunded Obligations of European Countries – Policy Report No.319*. Dallas, Texas: National Center for Policy Analysis, 2009.

Gono, G. '2012 Mid-Term Monetary Policy Statement', issued in terms of the Reserve Bank of Zimbabwe Act Chapter 22: 15, Section 46. Reserve Bank of Zimbabwe. 31 July 2012.

Greenspan, Alan. 'Gold and Economic Freedom'. This article originally appeared in a newsletter: 'The Objectivist' published in 1966 and was reprinted by Ayn Rand in *Capitalism: The Unknown Ideal*, New American Library1966.

Greenwald, Glenn. The NSA's mass and indiscriminate spying on Brazilians. *The Guardian*. 7 July 2013.

Hagino, Satoru and Sakuraba, Chihiro. *Measuring Government's Contingent Positions in Japan's Flow of Funds Accounts: Implications for GFSM*. Bank of Japan. 2011.

Hanke, Steve H and Krus, Nicholas, Nicholas. *World Hyperinflations – Cato Working Paper*. Washington DC: Cato Institute, August 2012.

Hanke, Steve H. *The Troubled Currencies Project*. Washington DC: CATO Institute, 2014. http://www.cato.org/research/troubled-currencies-project

Hartwig Lojsch, Rodríguez-Vives and Slavík, *The Size and Composition of Government Debt in the Euro Area*, European Central Bank Occasional Paper Series No 132, Frankfurt, 2011

Hayek, Friedrich A. *Prices and Production*. Augustus M. Kelly Publishers, 1935.

Hazlitt, Henry. *Economics in One Lesson*. Harper & Brothers, 1946.

Hazlitt, Henry. *The Inflation Crisis and How To Resolve It*. 1978.

Hazlitt, Henry. *What You Should Know About Inflation*. Princeton New Jersey: D Van Nostrand Company, Inc., 1965.

Herbener, Jeffrey M. 'After The Age of Inflation: Austrian Proposals for Monetary Reform'. *The Quarterly Journal of Austrian Economics*, Vol. 5, No. 4: 5–19, 2002.

Huerta de Soto, Jesús. *Money, Bank Credit, and Economic Cycles*. Auburn Alabama: Ludwig von Mises Institute, 2009.

Hülsmann, Jörg Guido. *The Ethics of Money Production*. Auburn Alabama: Ludwig von Mises Institute, 2008.

Hülsmann, Jörg Guido. *Theory of Money and Fiduciary Media: Essays in Celebration of the Centennial*. Auburn Alabama: Ludwig von Mises Institute, 2012.

IMF Country Report No. 03/225. *Zimbabwe: Selected Issues and Statistical Appendix*. Washington, DC: International Monetary Fund, July 2003.

IMF Country Report No. 05/359. *Zimbabwe: Selected Issues and Statistical Appendix*. Washington, DC: International Monetary Fund, October 2005.

IMF Country Report No. 09/139. *Staff Report for the 2009 Article IV Consultation*. Washington, DC: International Monetary Fund, May 2009.

IMF Country Report No. 12/279. *Zimbabwe: Staff Report for the 2012 Article IV Consultation*. Washington, DC: International Monetary Fund, September 2012.

IMF Staff Country Report No. 99/49. *Zimbabwe: Statistical Appendix*. Washington, DC: International Monetary Fund, June 1999.

Kiguel, Miguel A. 'Budget Deficits, Stability and the Monetary Dynmics of Hyperinflation'. *Journal of Money, Credit and Banking*, Vol. 21, No. 2, May 1989.

Lojsch, Dagmar Hartwig, Rodriguez-Vives, Marta and Slavik, Michal. *The Size And Composition Of Government Debt In The Euro Area – Occasional*

Paper Series No 132 / October 2011. Frankfurt, Germany: European Central Bank, 2011.

Marciano, Franscesca. *Rules of the Wild: A Novel of Africa*. UK and US: Vintage, 1998.

Maulden, John, and Tepper, Jonathan. *Endgame: The End of the Debt Supercycle and How It Changes Everything*. Hoboken, New Jersey: John Wiley & Sons Inc., 2011.

Mises, Ludwig von. *Human Action*. Fox & Wilkes, 1996.

Muñoz, Sònia. *Suppressed Inflation and Money Demand in Zimbabwe – IMF Working Paper WP/06/15*. Washington, DC: International Monetary Fund, 2006.

North, Gary. *Honest Money*. Fort Worth, Texas: Dominion Press, 1986.

Paul, Ron and Lehrman, Lewis. *The Case For Gold*. Washington DC: Cato Institute, 1982.

Raftopoulos, Brian and Mlambo, Alois. *Becoming Zimbabwe: A History from the Pre-colonial Period to 2008*. Johannesburg: Jacana Media, 2009.

Rickards, James. *Currency Wars: The Making of the Next Global Crisis*. New York: Penguin Group (USA) Inc., 2011.

Ritschl, Albrecht. *The Pity of Peace: Germany's Economy at War, 1914-1918 and Beyond*. Humboldt University Berlin and CEPR, 2005.

Rothbard, Murray N. *What Has Government Done to Our Money?* Auburn Alabama: Ludwig von Mises Institute, 1990.

Rothbard, Murray N. *A History of Money and Banking in the United States: The Colonial Era to World War II.* Auburn Alabama: Ludwig von Mises Institute, 2002.

Rothbard, Murray N. *The Mystery of Banking.* Auburn Alabama: Ludwig von Mises Institute, 2008.

Rothbard, Murray N. *Man, Economy, and State with Power and Market.* Auburn Alabama: Ludwig von Mises Institute, 2009.

Salerno, Joseph T. 'A Reformulation of Austrian Business Cycle Theory in Light of the Financial Crisis'. *The Quarterly Journal of Austrian Economics,* Vol. 15, No. 1, 2012.

Sargent, Thomas J. 'The Ends of Four Big Inflations' in *Inflation: Causes and Effects* by Robert E Hall, University of Chicago Press, 1982.

Saville, Adrian, Bader, Maureen and Spindler, Zane. 'Alternative Monetary Systems and the Quest for Stability: Can a Free Banking System Deliver in South Africa?' *South African Journal of Economics,* Vol. 73, No. 4, December 2005.

Stockman, David A. *The Great Deformation: The Corruption of Capitalism in America.* New York: Public Affairs, 2013.

Wiedemer, Robert. 'Money From Heaven' Is the Path to Hell. *Moneynews.* 8 December 2010.

Acknowledgements

Philip Haslam

Many thanks to those that who have come alongside and helped me make this a reality. Russ Lamberti, you have been a pillar of strength. What a great journey this has been. Thank you for your friendship. To the many people I interviewed whose heartfelt stories made this book come true, thank you. To my other co-labourers, Jason Goldberg and Cheryl-lyn Selman: you have helped me more than you know. To those who helped with my trip – Tim and Di, the Mhlanga's, Phil S, Carmen and Hazel R, thank you. To those who reviewed the book: Lauren S, Tandi H and Simon Watson. To Frans Nortje for the generous gift of a computer. To my Sinergi support. Joe A and Tandi H: thank you for the office. To Riaan Stoman and all at Pepperoni Pictures – your promo video rocks! To all those who provided strong and solid support along the way – Monique Mathys, Rich Wolfe, James Arthur, Grant Flaum, Neels Claasen, Dave 'the legend' Sales, Pedro de Jesus Ferreira, David Stone, Baggers, Bash, Schladers, JayZ, Fitz and MC, and Dad and Fran. My georgous, amazing, lovely wife, Bron. And finally, to my Heavenly Father. I'm humbled by all you have done.

Russell Lamberti

Thank you, Lord for planting in my heart the desire for monetary justice. Pam, thank you for being you, and for being 100% behind this project. You are my life partner in liberty. To Amber and Skyler – you both embody why I care about the future and want to help ensure it is a just, peaceful and prosperous one. Also, thanks for constantly reminding me what's truly important in life. To Dad, Ma, Nev, Amanda, Owen, Holly, Lisa, Chris, Tim, Paul, Dave, Delia, Jonty, Matt, Jen and Katherine – you all know why you matter so much. Chris Becks, I have one thing to say: vry. Thanks to George, Quin and ETM for everything you have done and will continue to do. To the New Creation family – I've learned so much from you all that finds expression in this book. And last but not least, to Phil Haslam. Well done, my friend. Thanks for opening the door to me on this project and leading it in dignity, humility, and honour.

About the Authors

Philip Haslam

Philip Haslam is an economic advisor, writer and speaker. Trained as a chartered accountant in South Africa, he furthered his career in finance and economics. As a speaker, he regularly presents to a variety of audiences on money, banking and the international financial system. His latest research into the Zimbabwe hyperinflation provides groundbreaking clues to the consequences of money printing. His goal is to influence multinational monetary policy with sound economic reform. Philip has lived in both Europe and America, and currently stays with his wife in his hometown of Johannesburg, South Africa.

Russell Lamberti

Russell Lamberti is chief strategist at an investment strategy consulting firm in South Africa. He consults to professional investors on economic policy, the money and banking system, international finance, business cycles and asset allocation. He is co-founder of the Ludwig von Mises Institute of South Africa, which promotes the market economy, private property, sound money, and peaceful international relations. Russell participates in roundtable discussion forums with senior monetary policy officials of the South African Reserve Bank. He is published in major news and financial publications and makes frequent television and radio appearances to discuss key topics on economics and financial markets. He has been a visiting lecturer to the Gordon Institute of Business Science MBA programme on fiscal and monetary policy. Russell lives with his wife and their children in Johannesburg, South Africa.

Russell and Philip started the *Monetary Justice Project*, which promotes monetary justice through advisory, advocacy, education, solution-building, and networking.

For further information about the services Russell and Philip offer, go to *WhenMoneyDestroys.com*. There, you'll be able to sign up to their regular mailer, find out the latest in global money printing and access other services.

To schedule a speaking engagement, obtain macro-economic consulting advice or to discuss any other query, consult the website.

Follow the authors on Twitter: *@HaslamPhilip* and *@RussLamberti*

Like their Facebook page: *www.facebook.com/whenmoneydestroys*

WhenMoneyDestroys.com

9 780620 590037